# LEVEL UP

## HOW TO
## ADVANCE IN
## YOUR CALLING AND
## NEVER GET STUCK

Level Up: How to Advance in Your Calling and Never Get Stuck
Copyright © 2024 by Chris Pace
Published by Messenger International
PO Box 888
Palmer Lake, CO 80133
MessengerInternational.org

Printed in the United States of America

All rights reserved. No part of this publication may be reproduced, stored in a retrieval system, or transmitted in any form or by any means without the prior written permission of the publisher. The only exception is brief quotations.

ISBN (978-1-937558-27-7)
ISBN (978-1-937558-28-4)
LCCN: 2023948953

Unless otherwise stated, all Scripture quotations are taken from the New King James Version. Copyright © 1982 by Thomas Nelson. Used by permission. All rights reserved. Scripture quotations marked (TPT) are taken from The Passion Translation®. Copyright © 2017 by BroadStreet Publishing® Group, LLC. Used by permission. All rights reserved. ThePassionTranslation.com. Scripture quotations marked (AMP) are taken from the Amplified Bible, Copyright © 2015 by The Lockman Foundation, La Habra, CA 90631. All rights reserved. Scripture quotations marked (NLT) are taken from the *Holy Bible*, New Living Translation, copyright © 1996, 2004, 2015 by Tyndale House Foundation. Used by permission of Tyndale House Publishers, Inc., Carol Stream, Illinois 60188. All rights reserved. Scripture quotations marked (MSG) are taken from The Message Bible, Copyright © 1993, 1994, 1995, 1996, 2000, 2001, 2002 by Eugene H. Peterson. Scripture quotations marked (AMPC) are taken from the Amplified Bible, Classic Edition, Copyright 1954, 1958, 1962, 1964, 1965, 1987 by The Lockman Foundation. Used by permission. www.Lockman.org. Scripture quotations marked (ESV) are taken from The Holy Bible, English Standard Version. ESV® Text Edition: 2016. Copyright © 2001 by Crossway Bibles, a publishing ministry of Good News Publishers. Scripture quotations marked (TLB) are taken from The Living Bible copyright © 1971 by Tyndale House Foundation. Used by permission of Tyndale House Publishers Inc., Carol Stream, Illinois 60188. All rights reserved. Except in quotations from the *Amplified Bible*, any italicization or words in brackets added to Scripture quotations are the author's additions for emphasis or clarity.

Edited by Bruce Nygren, Addison Bevere, Cory Emberson, and Laura Willbur.

Cover design by Joe Richardson.

*To Leonardo,*

*When your mother was pregnant with you, she bought me a journal and encouraged me to start recording life lessons for you.*

*Here are some of those lessons.*

*Dadda*

# CONTENTS

**FOREWORD**
by John Bevere    ix

## 1
### LEVELS
*Keep Progressing without Becoming Stuck!*    1

## 2
### NEXT UP
*Shift from Where You Have Potential to Where You Are Potent!*    11

## 3
### HIGHER PLACES
*Don't Settle for a Shallow Relationship with God When There Is More!*    23

## 4
### MAKE THE SHIFT
*It's Time to Meet God on His Level!*    33

## 5
### DOORS, WINDOWS, AND OPPORTUNITY
*A Sudden Good Break Can Change Everything!*    51

## 6
### REPOSITION YOURSELF
*When Things Have Changed, So Must You!*    69

## 7
### LEVERAGE YOUR LEVEL
*Preparation Time Is Never Wasted Time*    85

## 8
### UP YOUR GAME
*It's What You Do in the Dark That Makes You Shine in the Light*    103

## 9
### A HAND UP
*Mentors Will Help Move You from Where You Are to Where You Want to Go*    117

## 10
### NEW LEVELS, NEW DEVILS
*The Higher You Go, the Greater the Resistance You'll Face*    129

## 11
### PRAYER, POWER, AND BREAKTHROUGH
*Spiritual Victories Precede Physical Ones*    147

## 12
### THE ELEVATOR
*God Will Make a Way When There Seems No Way!*    163

**ACKNOWLEDGMENTS**    181

**ENDNOTES**    183

# FOREWORD

*By John Bevere*

Before I share my thoughts about this message, allow me to first share my heart about Chris, whom I've adopted as a spiritual son. I first met Chris in 2005 while I was on a ministry trip in Australia, and we have remained friends since. When we first met, I enjoyed his upbeat attitude and positive outlook on life. We often observe this in young believers, but sadly, watch it wane with time. Not with Chris! His enthusiasm is still contagious and electrifying. I'm convinced it is fueled by a genuine and deep love for Jesus Christ.

Chris worked in our Australian office, and in 2014 joined our World Headquarters in Colorado. In both locations, I've witnessed him serve in whatever capacity we asked. Not once has he refused or tried to get out of any task we put before him. Eventually, his communication abilities became evident to our leadership team. He is not only a gifted writer, but also an anointed teacher and preacher of God's Word. Over the years I've led Chris, I've watched him grow and navigate many tests and challenges—several of which could have caused him to abort his destiny. I'm so thankful he stayed the course!

At the start of 2020, I met with Chris and commissioned him to begin writing a book. Through prayer, I had sensed that he had a message inside of him that needed to come forth. And those who know me personally understand very well that this is not something I casually ask someone to do.

The message you now hold in your hands is a result of Chris remaining faithful to God and the calling on his life. Throughout the following pages, you'll discover that life is lived on levels, which also means that your calling is outworked through levels. When you fully grasp this truth, not only will you achieve all that God plans to accomplish in your present season, you'll also ensure your upward progress toward realizing your potential.

Your calling demands your full commitment. As you give yourself wholeheartedly to what God has called and gifted you to do, you'll not only level up; you'll make your life count, both now and for eternity. Regardless of your age or your accomplishments up until this point, you'll always have more to give and to contribute.

I'm so proud of Chris for writing this book. *Level Up* is a needed source of encouragement to strengthen and guide you along your upward journey. It will also equip you with the tools and insights required to advance in your calling and never get stuck. We have one shot at this life to give it everything we have. Let's hold nothing back, and let's be emptied, pouring ourselves out completely both in our service to others and as a gift to God.

I'm cheering you on as you Level Up and multiply your effectiveness!

>John Bevere
>Bestselling author and minister
>Co-founder of Messenger International

# 1

# LEVELS

*Keep Progressing without Becoming Stuck!*

"You're full of potential!"

I'm sure you've heard these words spoken over you before. Perhaps it was from a parent, a teacher, or a coach. As early as I could remember, my school report cards would always contain a short note: "Chris is full of potential." If I'm honest, it was a kind way for my teachers to inform my parents that I was underperforming.

When we consider this statement on our potential, we can conclude that it's one of the most encouraging things to hear; yet it's also one of the most discouraging things to hear—depending on when or how you hear it. On one hand, it's a statement packed with promise pointing to all you can be and have not yet become; all you can do and have not yet done. On the other hand, it's an indication that there's room for growth and improvement—that you're underperforming, not at the level you should be—just like my childhood report cards!

Perhaps later in life, we hit a point where we stop and begin to wonder why we're "here" and not "there." And by "there," I mean the expectations we had for ourselves. Life hasn't turned out the way we thought it would, and we often feel like we're once again reviewing a report card informing us that we're underperforming, or worse, failing. It can even feel like others have moved forward with their life while yours remains at a standstill. And it's in these moments when we must accept that it's not enough to be full of potential unless it is being realized.

Let's face it, one of the greatest tragedies in life is unfulfilled potential—all that could have been but never was. Sobering, isn't it?

In order to bridge the potential gap, we must first realize that everywhere we look, life is lived on levels. When I consider the concept of levels, I think of progression, like in physical growth, as we progress from childhood, to adolescence, to adulthood. We see levels in our education system, as we progress from elementary, to middle school, to high school, to college. The athletic system is played on levels, ranging from local, to state, to national. There are levels in leadership, government, and even video games! Homes and buildings are built on levels. And that's just the short list. Levels are everywhere you look.

Realizing our potential is a process of becoming, which is accomplished on levels. The benefit of progressing on levels is that we can grow incrementally, in phases and stages, allowing our growth to occur both organically and intentionally, rather than all at once.

So, before we move on, let's first establish what I mean by "level up." The best analogy I can think of is like that of leveling up in a video game. I don't consider myself a gamer, but I did play my fair share of video games as a child. (A big cowabunga to all my Ninja Turtles arcade fans!)

The goal of every level isn't just to win it, but to gain as much as you can from it. Within every level, there is always something to obtain or learn that you will need at a later time. Whether it's a hidden Easter egg, a special weapon, or golden coins—all of these items have a unique value and are often needed to help you both advance to the next level and function effectively within it. There are also items that help accelerate your progress, causing you to move forward in leaps and bounds. So, to level up means both to be equipped for the next level and to also advance to it.

Right now, you may not be where you want to be, but let me assure you: you're further along than you realize, and you're doing better than you think you are!

## An Upward Path

The path of life leads upward for the wise; they leave the grave behind. (Proverbs 15:24 NLT)

Our life is designed to have an upward trajectory. Every time you find yourself leveling up in life, you'll find yourself becoming more alive and energized, leaving the "grave" behind. That's because your potential was never meant to remain buried within you. I've often heard it said that if you're not progressing, you're regressing. And with every advancement to a new level, a new version of yourself will emerge.

Therefore, if we're wise, we'll follow God's paths which lead upward, paths that are uniquely designed to help us grow "stronger and stronger with every step forward" (Psalm 84:7 TPT). With this newfound strength, we too will discover, "The LORD God is my strength, and he will make my feet like hinds' feet, and he will make me to walk upon *mine high places*" (Habakkuk 3:19 KJV). Another translation says, "He makes my feet like hinds' feet and will make me to walk . . . and make [spiritual] progress upon my high places [of trouble, suffering, or responsibility]!" (AMPC).

So, we see that the "high places" we're called to refer to making spiritual progress that help us realize our potential—which at times will involve trouble and suffering.

In Hannah Hurnard's classic novel, *Hinds' Feet on High Places*, we find a great depiction of this upward journey that every child of God is invited to experience. This powerful allegory reveals the deep yearning we all possess for new heights of growth, adventure, and challenge.

The book reveals the spiritual journey of a timid young woman named Much-Afraid. Throughout her upward journey, Much-Afraid experiences life-defining moments as she navigates trouble, challenges, and the need to take responsibility for her growth. Along the way, she overcomes her tormenting fears and reaches the High Places, where she receives a new identity and experiences transformation.

The upward path, as Much-Afraid discovered, is a journey of becoming. Once again, realizing our potential occurs on levels. It doesn't happen in a moment; it happens with a culmination of moments. These moments must be maximized, and will require trust, courage, and a commitment to stay the course.

Similar to Much-Afraid, our upward journey will involve dangers and challenges, rewards and victory. Through it all, we'll not only grow closer to Jesus; we'll also awaken to our True Self and experience a transformation that's only possible as we embark on this upward path. But here's the reality: everyone is invited to the high places, yet not all of us accept this challenge.

I appreciate the stories of those, like the apostle Paul, who pursued their own upward journey. He wrote:

> Not that I have already attained, or am already perfected; but I press on, that I may lay hold of that for which Christ Jesus has also laid hold of me. Brethren, I do not count myself to have apprehended; but one thing I do, forgetting those things which are behind and reaching forward to those things which are ahead, I press toward the goal for the prize of the upward call of God in Christ Jesus. (Philippians 3:12–14)

Paul stated that his focus and passion was "the prize of the upward call." Everything he did was in pursuit of this goal, which was to know Jesus, become like Him, and fulfill the Lord's purpose for his life. But in order for Paul to reach the upward prize, he had to avoid settling for where he'd already been and what he'd already accomplished. He had to continue to level up—pressing onward and upward.

I've observed that many people don't reach the heights of their calling because they're not pressing toward it. They've settled for a lower level of living—one void of purpose, passion, and power. That's why I've written this book. I'm pursuing this upward call, because I want all that God has destined for me. And I desire the same for you.

Why settle for the low calling when the high calling is within your reach?

## Little by Little

God leads us into His plans and purposes on levels. This concept is clearly depicted in His dealings with the children of Israel, both the first and second generations, prior to entering the Promised Land. To the first generation, He explained:

> I will not drive them out from before you in one year, lest the land become desolate and the wild beasts multiply against you. *Little by little* I will drive them out from before you, until you have increased and possess the land. (Exodus 23:29–30 ESV)

Here we find the Lord leading the children of Israel forward little by little. We can also substitute "little by little" with "level by level." His strategy for leading them this way was to give them an opportunity to grow and increase, thus gaining strength for greater conquest. Unfortunately, that generation refused to enter the Promised Land due to their unbelief and disobedience.

This points out that our destiny is not automatic; we must step into it obediently, as the Lord leads. So, a whole generation died in the wilderness as the next generation arose. When it was time for them to possess the Promised Land, the Lord also explained:

> And the LORD your God will drive out those nations before you *little by little*; you will be unable to destroy them at once, lest the beasts of the field become *too* numerous for you. (Deuteronomy 7:22)

Again, the Lord leads His people forward "little by little" or "level by level."

This idea of progressing in levels is also observed in the New Testament. When Jesus described the kingdom, He would often use metaphors of growth and expansion that would occur on levels. Consider this example:

> And He said, "The kingdom of God is as if a man should scatter seed on the ground, and should sleep by night and rise by day, and the seed should sprout and grow, he himself does not know how. For the earth yields crops by itself: first the blade, then the head, after that the full grain in the head. (Mark 4:26–28)

Did you see that progression of growth on levels—first the blade, then the head, and after that, the full grain? Unless it's a miracle, everything occurs in levels, stages, and phases.

We live in a day and age in which we want it all and we want it now, but we fail to realize that we are living in a piece of God's overall plan for our lives right now—it's just unfolding gradually, little by little. We may not always see the big picture, but we will when we continue to grow and progress into our potential.

As we look back on our journey with God, I'm sure we're thankful that He's led us forward gradually. Think about it! If God, all at once, just dumped on us the full responsibility of all He's called us to do, we'd probably break! That's what God was indicating to the children of Israel when He said, "lest the beasts of the field become *too* numerous for you."

In other words, if He'd given them the Promised Land all at once, they would never have been able to handle it. It's the grace and mercy of God to lead us forward on levels.

## Promotion to Potential

When we think of advancing in levels, it's common to think of being promoted to a new position or rank. Although this is true, I'd like for us to rethink what we mean by "promotion," a word that has two primary meanings. The first is what we seek in our career, such as "being raised in position or rank."

In his book *The Peter Principle*, author Lawrence J. Peter observes that people in a hierarchy structure tend to rise to their level of incompetence. (Yes, you read that correctly!) Peter means that employees are frequently promoted based on their level of success in previous roles and positions, until they reach a level at which they are no longer competent, because skills in one job do not necessarily transfer well to another. For example, if a person is crushing it in a sales position, this does not guarantee success in the role of sales manager.

This leads us to the second definition for promotion, which is "furthering the growth or development of something." When a person is promoted to a new position, they have the capacity to grow in their new role. Even if they begin at a level of incompetence, they can still adapt and adjust to their new role and responsibilities. That encourages me, because it means I can not only *go to new levels*, but I can also *grow to new levels*. And that changes everything!

I like the term "promotion to potential." This is the core message of this book—*growing* to new levels, not just being promoted to new levels. It's worth repeating that realizing our potential is a process of becoming that is accomplished on levels.

If you've ever dreamed of being more than the person you presently are, or if you've ever envisioned yourself doing more than what you're doing now—then let's get started! You can begin taking strides toward those dreams today.

These strides will occur on levels.

Growing into new levels is necessary for your continued progression toward the upward call. And by the "upward call," I'm referring to God's purpose and plan for your life. Each of us is on a journey, and how we navigate our way determines how high we'll reach. Let's refuse to stay stuck and stagnant and, together, let's discover how to ascend by levels to the heights of our calling!

## CHEAT CODE

If we are to activate more of our "potential" on the upward path with God, we need to evaluate our progress on the journey. At the conclusion of each chapter, a short list of significant ideas to remember is added, as well as several reflection questions to help make what you're learning personal and practical. Take the time to fully benefit from the book's message by assessing your current level, and how—with the Spirit's help—you can "Level Up."

### Remember

- It's not enough to be full of potential—it must be realized.
- Personal growth occurs in levels.
- One of the greatest tragedies in life is unfulfilled potential.
- Destiny is not automatic; we must step into it obediently.

### Reflect

1. Are you progressing in your calling? In what ways have you felt stuck and frustrated?
2. How does understanding that life is lived on levels encourage you to keep growing?
3. In order for you to level up, what immediate action is required of you?

# 2

# NEXT UP

*Shift from Where You Have Potential to Where You Are Potent!*

*Potential* is a word packed with promise and carries with it the possibility of discovering more. But, if we are going to discover this more and realize all that we could become and do, we must move from where we have *potential* to where we are *potent*.

*Potent* is another word which I love that means "having great power or effect."[1] The Merriam-Webster Dictionary states that it means "achieving or bringing about a particular result." My personal definition is "present-tense power." A person who is potent is a person who is realizing their potential—alive with purpose, passion, and power. Therefore, potent is a posture that positions you to come alive.

The words of civil rights leader Howard Thurman capture the beauty of this potent posture: "Don't ask what the world needs. Ask what makes you come alive and go do it. Because what the world needs are people who have come alive."

It's time to come alive.

## Activation

To transition from where we have potential to where we are potent, our potential must be activated. Triggering our untapped ability begins with an awakening followed by action, acquisition, and association, all of which lead to actualization. These stages are not one-offs but are cyclical throughout each level of life. Let's briefly dive into each of these areas. (As a side note, we'll also further explore these concepts in other chapters.)

### Awakening

Potential is connected to purpose. When you discover your purpose, you can begin to unlock your potential. There are many ways these moments of awakening can happen, but they all originate from God, whether through a sovereign interruption or by diligent seeking.

Here's something I've learned about hearing God: pay attention to what is happening within you. Our hearts know things that our minds don't. Unless it has been suppressed, each of us are gripped by a sense of divine purpose that mysteriously guides and directs our paths. We know deep down that we are here on purpose for a purpose. Solomon recorded, "He has also planted eternity [a sense of divine purpose] in the human heart [a mysterious longing which nothing under the sun can satisfy, except God]" (Ecclesiastes 3:11 AMP).

These moments of awakening often resonate with what our hearts know to be true, even if it doesn't immediately make sense to our minds. That's because God shapes His will in us far more than He speaks His will to us: "For it is . . . God who is effectively at work in you, both to will and to work [that is, strengthening, energizing, and creating in you the longing and the ability to fulfill your purpose] for His good pleasure" (Philippians 2:13 AMP).

In Acts 7:23, we're told of Moses's moment of awakening to his purpose: "Now when he was forty years old, *it came into his heart* to visit his brethren, the children of Israel." Notice the words "it came into his heart." An awakening occurred, and Moses began shifting from where he had potential to where he was potent.

In the following verses, we're told how he killed an Egyptian who was mistreating an Israelite and how he also tried to break up a fight between two Hebrew men (v. 23-29). Moses's potential as Israel's deliverer was beginning to be realized, even though the timing was a little off and no one could recognize it at the time (see Acts 7:23-36). Moses, nonetheless, was coming alive. His life would take on new meaning. Purpose had been awakened, and he would never be the same.

As we've seen, people who have come alive are those who have discovered their purpose, which, as a result, ignites their passion and activates their potential. Moses's moment was by an act of sovereignty, but you do not have to wait for moments like that—you can also seek them out.

> It's in Christ that we find out who we are and what we are living for. Long before we first heard of Christ and got our hopes up, he had his eye on us, had designs on us for glorious living, part of the overall purpose he is working out in everything and everyone. (Ephesians 1:11-12 MSG)

Through diligently seeking the Lord—the one who knows the plans and designs He has for you—you, too, can awaken to your purpose and begin your upward journey—taking your place and playing your part in God's overall plan for humanity. (I share more about this in the chapters titled *Higher Places* and *Make the Shift*.)

### Action

Once you become aware of your purpose, you also become aware of your potential. They are closely related. This awakening necessitates action. Because once you come alive with purpose, passion is sparked to fuel your pursuit of it—which, as I've already stated, enables you to realize your potential and level up into God's plans and purposes for your life.

One of the reasons people fail to act is because they are expecting God to do everything for them. In turn, they fail to take responsibility for their lives. And, as a result, they disempower themselves and become victims of external forces, waiting to be seen and picked.

Seth Godin articulated this perfectly:

> "The opportunity of a lifetime is to pick yourself. Quit waiting to get picked; quit waiting for someone to give you permission; quit waiting for someone to say you are officially qualified and pick yourself. It doesn't mean you have to be an entrepreneur or a freelancer, but it does mean you stand up and say, 'I have something to say. I know how to do something. I'm doing it. If you want me to do it with you, raise your hand.'"

Picking yourself doesn't mean you become a lone ranger and ride alone. Picking yourself looks more like believing in yourself, believing in what God has given you and not waiting for the validation of others. Look at what the apostle Paul shared:

> Make a careful exploration of who you are and the work you have been given, and then sink yourself into that. Don't be impressed with yourself. Don't compare yourself with others. Each of you must take responsibility for doing the creative best you can with your own life. (Galatians 6:4–5 MSG)

Agency and action go hand in hand. Unless you take responsibility for exploring your identity and purpose, your potential will remain hidden and unknown. To be responsible means to be answerable or accountable for something within one's power, control, or management. It's doing the things you are supposed to do and accepting the results of your actions.

A person is most potent when they take responsibility for their own life. Begin taking action, and fully immerse yourself in doing the creative best you can with the gifts, resources, and opportunities you've been given. More seems to happen when we proactively move into the future rather than simply letting life happen. And each step of obedience you take is like a puzzle piece. As the pieces come together, the big picture is made clear. (I share more on this in the chapters titled *Reposition Yourself* and *Doors, Windows, and Opportunity*.)

## Acquisition

In the previous chapter, I used the analogy of a virtual video game to describe what I mean by leveling up. Remember, the goal of every level isn't just to simply get through it, but to gain as much as you can from it. Within every level, there is always something to obtain or learn that you will need later.

Along our upward path, we need to be consistently acquiring skills, knowledge, and experiences that are unique and necessary to fulfill our purpose and realize our potential. (I share more about this in the chapters titled *Leverage Your Level* and *Up Your Game*.)

## Associations

Another thing that helps activate our potential are relationships—those we surround ourselves with along the upward path. These relationships greatly influence the trajectory of our lives and our development into our potential. They have the ability to see aptitudes and abilities in us that we're not even aware of. (I share more about this in the chapter titled *A Hand Up*.)

## Actualization

One of the greatest rewards in life is growing into your potential and actualizing God's plans and purposes for your life. On the flip side, one of the greatest tragedies in life is unfulfilled potential—not realizing all that God had destined for you. Innumerable individuals have robbed the world of their God-given talents and abilities by taking them to the grave—undeveloped and unrealized.

Citing Howard Thurman once again, consider this riveting allegory he used that brings perspective to what we're discussing:

"Imagine, if you will, being on your deathbed, and standing around your bed are the ghosts of the ideas, the abilities, the talents, the gifts, the dreams given to you by life. That you, for whatever reason, never pursued those dreams. You never did anything with those ideas. You never used those talents. You never used those gifts. You never took advantage of those opportunities. And there they are, standing around your bed, looking at you before you take your last dying breath, looking at you with angry eyes saying, 'We came to you, and only you could have given us life and now we must die with you forever.'"

Sobering, isn't it? If you died today, what dreams, desires, and ideas would die with you? What gifts and abilities would remain unknown and undeveloped? What knowledge and insights would be buried forever? What about the people whose lives will not be impacted by what you had to offer? Or worse, what do you think it would be like when you're standing before Christ at the Judgment Seat giving an account of the way you stewarded what was entrusted to you?

Remember: it's not enough to be full of potential . . . unless it's being realized.

## Are You Passive or Potent?

Ben Stiller's *The Secret Life of Walter Mitty* is one of my all-time favorite movies. The story's hero, Walter Mitty, is a daydreamer—a *LIFE* Magazine employee who spends his days in the company's basement reviewing negatives and developing photos—desperate to escape his mundane existence through a fantasy world filled with heroism, romance, and adventure.

Early in the movie, Walter receives a call from Todd, an eHarmony employee who calls to question him about the "been there, done that" section of his online dating profile. After an awkward pause, Walter confesses to having nothing noteworthy to mention—a response that clearly depicts his life up until that moment. A life many settle for—existing rather than truly living.

But as the movie progresses, so does Walter. We watch him rise above passivity and shift from where he has potential to where he becomes potent. And it's nothing short of inspirational! Walter grows from a dreamer to a risk-taker—cycling toward active volcanoes, jumping off helicopters into shark-infested waters, and winning the heart of the woman of his dreams! His transformation is undeniable. And it's a transformation that's possible for anyone brave enough to grow into their potential.

Can you relate to Walter? Perhaps you dream of who you could become and what you could accomplish but lack the courage and resolve to move in that direction? If you were asked about your "been there, done that" section, what would you share?

What do your answers reveal about your life? Are you living a passive or a potent life?

### Release Your Potential

Before we move on, let's look at what stifles and suppresses your potential, leaving you in a state of slumber. In his second letter to the believers at Corinth, the apostle Paul empathetically spoke to a dilemma that hinders many from leveling up:

> Dear, dear Corinthians, I can't tell you how much I long for you to enter this wide-open, spacious life. We didn't fence you in. The smallness you feel comes from within you. Your lives aren't small, but you're living them in a small way. I'm speaking as plainly as I can and with great affection. Open up your lives. Live openly and expansively! (2 Corinthians 6:11–13 MSG)

The key word here is *expansively*, which describes having a life with the capacity to grow and expand in order to reach your maximum potential. The opposite of this is to live a life that's confined and limited. Are you living your life in a small way—limited and fenced in? Is it time for you to begin living openly and expansively?

A simple example is the term "pot-bound," which is used to describe a houseplant that's outgrown its pot. Symptoms of such a plant are stunted growth, frequent wilting, smaller new leaves, poor quality of flowers, and limited space for root spread and expansion. For a pot-bound plant to survive and reach its potential growth, it must be removed from its small pot into a more spacious container.

Living your life in a small way means you're not growing into your potential. If we want to avoid stunting our growth and becoming "pot-bound," we need to open up our life and live expansively. This involves obediently following God along the upward journey as we grow, mature, develop, deepen our roots, and bear more fruit.

Throughout the Bible, you'll find those God called living their lives in a small way—that is, until He opened their lives to purpose. At the root of this smallness was inferiority—that persistent sense of feeling small, unimportant, powerless, and inadequate.

Moses's inferiority was rooted in his speech impediment, and he kept raising objections to God, even pleading with Him to send someone else: "Master, please, I don't talk well. I've never been good with words, neither before nor after you spoke to me. I stutter and stammer . . . Oh, Master, please! Send somebody else!" (Exodus 4:10, 13 MSG).

Gideon was another who struggled with inferiority. His was rooted in his social and family status: "But how can I rescue Israel? My clan is the weakest one in Manasseh, and everyone else in my family is more important than I am" (Judges 6:15 CEV).

David's struggle was like Gideon's. When Saul brought him to the palace, he responded, "How could I possibly marry your daughter? I'm not very important, and neither is my family" (1 Samuel 18:18 CEV). Both Gideon and David viewed themselves as insignificant.

One of the most unforgettable accounts is that of the spies who were sent out to scout the Promised Land. Their sense of inferiority disabled them, and they forfeited their destiny: "We felt as small as grasshoppers and that is how we must have looked to them!" (Numbers 13:33 CEV).

Think about these accounts. With each one of them, God was about to take them to new levels of purpose, which would also cause them to realize greater levels of potential—enabling them to discover strength they never knew they had and to accomplish things they never knew they could do.

Some did. Others didn't.

What will you do?

These words by Marianne Williamson have been a source of strength for me. I'd like to share them with you:

> Our deepest fear is not that we are inadequate. Our deepest fear is that we are powerful beyond measure. It is our light, not our darkness that most frightens us. We ask ourselves, 'Who am I to be brilliant, gorgeous, talented, fabulous?' Actually, who are you not to be? You are a child of God. Your playing small does not serve the world. There is nothing enlightened about shrinking so that other people won't feel insecure around you. We are all meant to shine, as children do. We were born to make manifest the glory of God that is within us. It's not just in some of us; it's in everyone. And as we let our own light shine, we unconsciously give other people permission to do the same. As we are liberated from our own fear, our presence automatically liberates others."

My prayer and hope are that you'll be like those who, despite their insecurities and inadequacies, chose to overcome themselves so they could become better versions of themselves. No one can get you out of God's will for your life except you. And honestly, we can often be our own worst enemy. So, don't sabotage your destiny just because you don't feel good enough. Become good enough!

## Next Up

One area in which advancement to new levels is evident is professional sports. I'm an avid NBA fan, and one of my favorite events every year (other than the NBA playoffs) is the NBA draft. As I once had hoop dreams of my own, I used to imagine my name being called by the commissioner as the number-one pick (or at least a top-three pick). Ugh . . . if only I had been a bit taller!

Draft day is a big day for team owners and general managers looking to rebuild or strengthen their rosters. Extensive scouting and research have been invested in drafting the right players. Throughout the years, this has included prospects like Shaquille O'Neal, LeBron James, and Zion Williamson—rising stars since middle school that had coaches drooling. A common term spoken over these up-and-comers is, "Next Up," an idiom The Urban Dictionary defines as, "When someone or something is on the verge of blowing up and becoming really successful." It's like saying, "Keep an eye on this one; you're going to hear more about him in the near future!"

Highly touted prospects at the collegiate level don't always meet expectations at the pro level. They become draft busts! For example, do you remember Sam Bowie? If not—he's the guy drafted number two by the Portland Trailblazers in the 1984 draft . . . one spot ahead of a guy named Michael Jordan, who was third overall. (Ouch! A bad day for the Trailblazers!)

Why is a player a bust? There are many reasons, but the most common is that they fail to make the necessary adjustments to compete at the pro level. On the contrary, many college players who are not considered "the cream of the crop" and were not high draft picks have excelled in the pros. What made the difference? And how does this apply to us in our sphere of influence?

We'll discuss the answers to these questions and much more throughout this book. But for now, we can conclude that high potential does not always equate to high performance. And success on one level does not guarantee success at the next. This is why it's not enough to be full of potential. We must be committed to leveling up into it.

## Courage Is Calling

Recently, I read about a man who had a recurring dream of a lion chasing him until he would fall over exhausted, trying to escape. Without fail, he'd wake up sweating profusely and with his heart racing. Desperate for answers, this man met with his pastor, hoping to understand what this recurring dream meant. They discussed potential meanings of what the lion could represent—his boss, his wife, the devil, etc.—but none of these explanations resonated with either of them.

After an hour of discussion, the pastor suggested they pray. As they did, he asked the man to recall the dream in his mind, and instead of running away from the lion, he instructed the man to stand still and ask the lion who he is and what he wants.

When the time came for the man to confront the lion, he found himself face to face with it. As the lion stood there, sniffing and snorting, the man asked, "Who are you?" To his amazement, the lion responded, "I am your courage and your strength. Why are you running away from me?"

This dream resonated with me so much, as it perfectly conveys the idea of moving from where we have potential to where we are potent. We need not be afraid of our potential—who we're capable of becoming and what we're capable of accomplishing. Of course, this journey of becoming is scary, and will no doubt require courage. But I encourage you to be more afraid of regret than you are of risk.

Your playing small does not serve the world. Courage is calling for you. It's time to shift from where you have potential to where you are potent.

You're next up!

# CHEAT CODE

### Remember
- A person who is potent is a person who is realizing their potential—alive with purpose, passion, and power. Therefore, potent is a posture that positions you to come alive.
- To transition from where we have potential to where we are potent, our potential must be activated.
- Our hearts know things that our minds don't.
- A person is most potent when they take responsibility for their own life.

### Reflect
1. Are you taking responsibility for doing the creative best you can with your own life?
2. In what areas of your life are you passive instead of potent? What needs to change?
3. Are you waiting to be picked and given permission by others to pursue your purpose? If so, why?

# 3

# HIGHER PLACES

*Don't Settle for a Shallow Relationship with God When There Is More!*

The upward journey begins and ends with God.

Ascending to the heights of our upward call begins with becoming acquainted with the One who leads us there. He is, after all, the Author and Finisher of this path set before us. Therefore, we'll need His involvement as we navigate its terrain. Without His guidance, we'll only travel in circles around our mountain rather than ascend it.

Listen to this wonderful promise we've been given:

> "I hear the Lord saying, 'I will stay close to you, instructing and guiding you along the pathway for your life. I will advise you along the way and lead you forth with my eyes as your guide. So don't make it difficult; don't be stubborn when I take you where you've not been before. Don't make me tug you and pull you along. Just come with me!'" (Psalm 32:8-9 TPT)

The best way to never miss God is to walk with God. It's really simple but often overlooked. And the reality is, you and I are as close to God as we have chosen to be. I know this can be hard to hear, but we determine our level of relationship with God, not Him. He's already made a way for us to enter His presence, and the nearness to Him that we seek will determine the level of relationship we'll have with Him. And the closer we are, the more we'll sense His nearness and guidance.

When I feel disconnected from God, it's often because I've been distant and haven't spent quality time with Him. Or, as the Psalmist pointed out in the verses above, it's often our own stubbornness that makes following God difficult. With any committed relationship, it takes intentionality to cultivate intimacy and build understanding. In relation to this, Paul wrote:

> [For my determined purpose is] that I may know Him [that I may progressively become more deeply and intimately acquainted with Him, perceiving and recognizing and understanding the wonders of His Person more strongly and more clearly].... (Philippians 3:10 AMPC)
> For now we see in a mirror, dimly, but then face to face. Now I know in part, but then I shall know just as I also am known. (1 Corinthians 13:12)

Becoming more deeply and intimately acquainted with the Lord is a lifelong journey that progresses in levels—beginning with seeing Him dimly and moving up to seeing Him face to face; from knowing Him partially, to knowing Him as He knows us. As we grow in our knowledge of God, we'll also advance to new levels of relationship. The writer of Hebrews reveals the secret of ascending to new heights with the Lord:

> But without faith *it is* impossible to please *Him,* for he who comes to God must believe that He is, and *that* He is a rewarder of those who diligently seek Him. (Hebrews 11:6)

The pursuit of God requires both determination and diligence. Paul's determined purpose first and foremost was to know God. Your priorities are seen in what you pursue. That's why pursuing God must be done diligently. The word "diligent" implies a constant and persistent effort to accomplish something. In this case, it's an effort to know God. When this diligence is applied, God will reward you with His presence, which is the God-chaser's ultimate reward!

With this in mind, I'm sure your heart has been ignited with a passion to know God more! And that's how this pursuit begins—with a heart that burns with the conviction that God exists and that He can be known in personal experience. It's this faith to lay hold of God that fuels a diligent seeking of Him. And God has promised through Jeremiah, "Then [with a deep longing] you will seek Me and require Me [as a vital necessity] and [you will] find Me when you search for Me with all your heart" (Jeremiah 29:13 AMP).

## Stairway to Heaven

Throughout the Scriptures, we see people engaged with God on a variety of levels. Examples in the Old Testament include Moses and the Israelites. During the time God was gathering the children of Israel out of Egypt and to Himself in the wilderness, He established four different levels of relationships. There were certain parameters and boundaries put in place when the Lord descended upon Mount Sinai.

The first level was at the foot of the mountain, where all the children of Israel could worship the Lord from a safe distance. Sadly, even today this is where many believers live; they're near enough to feel a sense of closeness to God, but far enough away so they can still live as they please. This level became evident when Moses came down from the mountain and found the Israelites "playing church" and worshipping the golden calf that Aaron had created for them.

To the second level, only Aaron, Nadab, Abihu, and seventy of the elders of Israel were allowed to advance. They were all privileged to see glimpses of the God of Israel. Again, most of these leaders were eventually found at the base of the mountain with the rest of the Israelites "playing church" and worshipping the golden calf. I believe this is symbolic of church services and conferences now in which we experience the presence and power of God in an extraordinary way. These moments of outpouring and impartation are powerful and refreshing, but not enough to sustain a life-giving relationship with the Lord.

Apart from the seventy others, Moses and Joshua were called higher—to the third level—in which they drew even closer to God. This level is where encountering God in a corporate setting is not enough—God chasers must have *more*, which comes from personal encounters and experiences apart from the crowd. At this level, transformation of the heart occurs.

That's why Joshua often was found staying as close as possible to the presence of God, even when Moses and others had left (see Exodus 33:10–11). Individuals at this level are not content to just witness the works of God: they must also understand the ways of God, which comes from knowing His heart and spending quality time with Him.

From this level, Joshua witnessed Moses enter the fourth level, where within the cloud he entered the very presence of God. No wonder Moses remained there for forty days and forty nights. Within that place, the Lord spoke to him face to face and gave him the Ten Commandments (see Exodus 19:9–12; Exodus 24:9–17).

This highest level requires a commitment that not many are willing to make. It demands a complete giving of yourself to the Lord and His will for your life. At this level, extended periods of lingering in God's presence, fasting, and prayer are necessary, awakening a greater awareness and desire for God Himself.

In the New Testament, we find the four levels again with those who followed Jesus. We see that Jesus appointed approximately seventy people to join His ministry team and travel ahead of Him to all the cities and places where He'd planned to go (see Luke 10:1). From those seventy followers, Jesus selected twelve disciples to share a deeper relationship with Him. Out of the twelve, three—Peter, James, and John—were brought even closer to experience things with Jesus that the others did not. Then, out of the three, John drew even closer, becoming His closest confidant.

So, we see clearly, from both the Old and New Testaments, that we are as close to God as we choose to be. I cannot emphasize this point enough. *God doesn't play favorites.* All His sons and daughters can know Him intimately, if they choose to seek Him.

Is it time to take your relationship with God to new levels?

## Come Up Higher

For us to ascend to new levels with the Lord, we must first be aware of the place we hold in the spirit realm along with the access we've already been given. As believers, we are seated with Jesus in heavenly places (see Ephesians 2:6). We hold a position with Him "far above any ruler or authority or power or leader or anything else—not only in this world but also in the world to come" (Ephesians 1:21 NLT).

With this vantage, we're given access to the Most High, and we're positioned to see things differently, as we are given heavenly vision and perspective. With this in mind, take a look at invitations from both Jesus and Paul to level up in our relationship with God:

> Then as I looked, I saw a door standing open in heaven, and the same voice I had heard before spoke to me like a trumpet blast. The voice said, "Come up here, and I will show you what must happen after this." And instantly I was in the Spirit, and I saw a throne in heaven and someone sitting on it. (Revelation 4:1–2 NLT)
>
> So, if you're serious about living this new resurrection life with Christ, *act* like it. Pursue the things over which Christ presides. Don't shuffle along, eyes to the ground, absorbed with the things right in front of you. Look up, and be alert to what is going on around Christ—that's where the action is. See things from *his* perspective. (Colossians 3:1–2 MSG)

Both these statements urge us to come up higher—to live from a higher position already provided for us. It's a reminder not to become so absorbed with the day-to-day things that occupy our time and energy that we become oblivious to God. When we learn how to live with a heaven-to-earth perspective, day-to-day life is energized with heaven's realities, transforming the way we live. Living from this higher place will make us more "heavenly minded" so that we can be more "earthly good."

Are you content at the foot of the mountain? Or are you ready to make the climb?

Jesus modeled what living from heaven to earth looks like. In John 3, Jesus is engaged in a conversation about being born again with a respected Jewish leader named Nicodemus. During their talk, because his understanding was limited, Nicodemus struggled to comprehend the truths Jesus was sharing. Jesus marveled at this, because Nicodemus should have known better—he was a Pharisee and a teacher of the law. So, why the disconnect? Jesus explains:

> "If I have told you earthly things and you do not believe, how will you believe if I tell you heavenly things? No one has ascended to heaven but He who came down from heaven, *that is,* the Son of Man who is in heaven." (John 3:12–13)

Two important insights from these verses: First, Jesus differentiates between two types of wisdom—"earthly things" and "heavenly things"—with heavenly wisdom definitely superseding earthly wisdom.

God's ways are higher than our ways.

His thoughts are higher than our thoughts.

God's wisdom and ways are on a much higher level than the world's—a significant example being the mystery and wonder of our opportunity to be born again.

Second, Jesus locates Himself in both heaven and earth. They're subtle, but go over His words again in the verses above from John. We know that He came down from heaven, but He also states that He, "the Son of Man," is in heaven. So, while visiting with Nicodemus, was Jesus on earth or in heaven? Obviously, He was on earth. What I believe that

Jesus was indicating is that He lived from heaven to earth. Positionally, as we do now according to Scripture, Jesus occupied a place of authority in heaven while living practically on earth.

Unless we, too, learn to live from this higher realm, we'll struggle—just like Nicodemus—to understand God's higher ways and wisdom. And we'll fail to effectively bring heaven to earth.

Thankfully, the Lord has given us His Spirit who enables us to have constant access to this higher realm. Once again, ponder these wonderful promises revealed from both Jesus and Paul concerning the Holy Spirit's involvement in our life:

> "I still have many things to say to you, but you cannot bear *them* now. However, when He, the Spirit of truth, has come, He will guide you into all truth; for He will not speak on His own *authority*, but whatever He hears He will speak; and He will tell you things to come. He will glorify Me, for He will take of what is Mine and declare *it* to you." (John 16:12–14)

> But as it is written: "Eye has not seen, nor ear heard, nor have entered into the heart of man the things which God has prepared for those who love Him." But God has revealed them to us through His Spirit. For the Spirit searches all things, yes, the deep things of God. For what man knows the things of a man except the spirit of the man which is in him? Even so no one knows the things of God except the Spirit of God. Now we have received, not the spirit of the world, but the Spirit who is from God, that we might know the things that have been freely given to us by God. These things we also speak, not in words which man's wisdom teaches but which the Holy Spirit teaches, comparing spiritual things with spiritual. But the natural man does not receive the things of the Spirit of God, for they are foolishness to him; nor can he know *them*, because they are spiritually discerned. (1 Corinthians 2:9–14)

Jesus still has many things to say to us. Through the help of His Spirit, we can both hear and understand the heavenly things reserved for us. Through the Holy Spirit, we have been given access to the heart and mind of God. He leads us into all truth and reveals to us heavenly things that can only be understood by His assistance.

But there is a clause: only those who are spiritual can be on the same frequency as God's Spirit. Recall Paul's words concerning the Holy Spirit, as he teaches, "comparing spiritual things with those who are spiritual." That is, as The Message paraphrases it beautifully, "The unspiritual self, just as it is by nature, can't receive the gifts of God's Spirit. There's no capacity for them. They seem like so much silliness. Spirit can be known only by spirit—God's Spirit and our spirits in open communion. Spiritually alive, we have access to everything God's Spirit is doing."

The Passion Translation describes it this way: "Someone living on an entirely human level rejects the revelations of God's Spirit, for they make no sense to him. He can't understand the revelations of the Spirit because they are only discovered by the illumination of the Spirit."

So, we see clearly there are levels—the lower level being carnally minded and the higher level being spiritually minded. Paul continues in the next chapter, sharing, "Brothers and sisters, when I was with you, I found it impossible to speak to you as those who are spiritually mature people, for you are still dominated by the mind-set of the flesh. And because you are immature infants in Christ, I had to nurse you and feed you with "milk," not with the solid food of more advanced teachings, because you weren't ready for it" (1 Corinthians 3:1–3 TPT).

These words sound similar to what Jesus shared with His disciples: "I still have many things to say to you, but you cannot bear them now." Both Jesus and Paul wanted to share more advanced knowledge, but it required spiritual maturity—leveling up from being "carnally minded" to being "spiritually minded." The writer of Hebrews adds, "But solid food is for the mature, whose spiritual senses perceive heavenly matters" (Hebrews 5:14 TPT).

Could this be why some people seem to hear from God more than others? (We'll dive deeper on this in the next chapter.)

The Holy Spirit is the game-changer. Think about the possibilities this opens up to us in our spheres of influence. Think about the insights and know-how He can provide so that we can distinguish ourselves and live life on new levels. If we're tapping into the unlimited resources available to us through our relationship with God's Spirit, we really have an unfair advantage among our peers. Heaven is always available as God's Spirit unveils our eyes to things unseen and opens our ears to things unheard—giving us access to His infinite knowledge and storehouse of wisdom.

So, having established that God can be known on levels, let's now turn our attention to how we can make the necessary shifts.

## CHEAT CODE

### Remember
- "We are as close to God as we choose to be."
- "Pursuit of God requires both determination and diligence."
- There are levels of relationship with God; only those who hunger and thirst reach the heights.
- The Holy Spirit is the "game-changer" in developing a deeper relationship with God.

### Reflect
1. "We are as close to God as we choose to be." What choices do you need to make now to have a more intimate relationship with God?
2. How might you allow the Holy Spirit to be more of a "game-changer" in your life?

# 4

# MAKE THE SHIFT

*It's Time to Meet God on His Level!*

Now that we know we're not bound to the earth, how can we make the shift to live with God from this higher level?

In the aftermath of the terrorist attacks on New York's World Trade Center Towers in 2001, I found myself examining my life and questioning my purpose—feeling as if my beliefs and perspectives also had come tumbling down on 9/11. As an Australian not living in America and watching from afar, it seemed like I had stumbled into a horror movie. I was gripped by fear and uncertainty, as were many around the world. During that time, I began to diligently seek God.

Some months later in 2002, my older cousin, Richard, who is a pastor, led me to Jesus and began discipling me. I was living in Sydney, and I had chosen to postpone attending college so I could reevaluate the direction my life was heading. Those early days as a new believer were precious to me. Hours were spent immersing myself in the Bible and listening to sermons. Although there was a lot to wrap my head around, I was eager to learn more about God and Scripture.

In 2003, my life drastically changed when my parents, who also had become Christians, invited my brother, Jay, and me to attend an event hosted by an evangelist from India. I had no idea the impact this moment would have on my life.

At the first session, my brother and I arrived late, and we sat in the back. The venue was almost filled to capacity, and the many hundreds were engaged in praise and worship. I looked around, hoping to locate my parents. As I surveyed the crowd, my eyes fixed on an elderly woman standing a few feet away from us. The lady was praying for a couple in the crowd. While she prayed, she shook and spoke in a foreign language. I was mesmerized.

The meeting became a blur. I didn't really understand much of what the preacher shared, except that he cried a lot and often shook his fist in the air. When the service was over, I turned to my brother to make plans to eat. Suddenly, I felt a hand grip my shoulder. As I turned around, I was surprised to find the elderly woman I'd seen earlier standing behind me.

"Hello, young man," she said.

"Um . . . hi," I replied.

"Can I pray for you and your friend?" she asked.

"Sure," I answered. "He's actually my brother."

She laid her hands on us and began to pray. Several minutes went by, and I began to shake with what felt like electric pulses vibrating through my body. The vibrations began slowly, and then intensified, until I was shaking uncontrollably. No matter how much I tried to stop trembling, I couldn't. Then I heard the elderly woman speak these words over me: "Jesus is touching you right now, and you're going to receive a visitation from the Lord soon."

The drive home that night was a little awkward. My brother drove while I sat in the passenger seat feeling inebriated as the vibrations slowly diminished. I remained silent, attempting to comprehend what had taken place at the meeting.

Two weeks later, I had a visitation from the Lord. It happened between the hours of two and three o'clock in the morning. I sat up in bed and threw off my blanket. I took a few deep breaths while wondering why I had awakened so abruptly. After a couple of minutes, I laid back down, hoping to fall asleep. As soon as my face touched my pillow, I heard a sudden rip in the atmosphere and a swirling, mighty, ferocious wind hovering above me.

Immediately, I tried to leap out of bed . . . but I couldn't move. I was pinned! In that moment, I could differentiate between my spirit, my soul, and my body. My spirit was at peace, quietly anticipating something. Thoughts raced through my mind like a movie reel. As for my body, it wanted to flee!

While I lay there, helpless, the loud, swirling wind moved away from me. Then it circled back, hitting my chest like a hurricane. Joy filled my heart as the wind entered me. Then I heard a trumpet blast and an angelic voice declare, "The Spirit of the Lord is upon you!" This voice was unlike anything I'd ever heard before. It was both magnificent and authoritative—not of this world! What was interesting was that it sounded as if the voice and the trumpet were intertwined, sounding as one.

Once the words were uttered, I was able to spring out of bed, trembling. All I could mutter was, "Holy . . . Holy . . . Holy Spirit." I immediately thought of Acts Chapter 2: "And suddenly there came a sound from heaven, as of a rushing mighty wind, and it filled the whole house where they were sitting" (verse 2).

From that moment on, I was never the same. Jesus became real to me. The Scriptures came alive. And all I wanted to do was pray and become better acquainted with God. I've lost count of how many times I've shared this story with others. Each time I do, I receive the same reaction—jaws drop and eyes open wide! If anything, my story creates a hunger in others to know God in a more real and tangible way—you know, the stuff we read about in the Bible! Things like Paul's encounter on the road to Damascus (Acts 9), or his third-heaven experience, which he even hesitated to talk about (2 Corinthians 12:1–4).

Honestly, I could write at length about the numerous God encounters mentioned throughout Scripture. And my response to them is the same as when I share my story with others—holy jealousy! My point is that these experiences exist, and that you, too, can encounter God in a real and tangible way. Such personal encounters with God are necessary if a shift from just "Bible stories" to similar experiences to mine are to occur. Otherwise, you'll only know God in theory, not experientially. But don't take my word for it; here's what Jesus said:

> "You are busy analyzing the Scriptures, frantically poring over them in hopes of gaining eternal life. Everything you read points to me, yet you still refuse to come to me so I can give you the life you're looking for—eternal life!" (John 5:39–40 TPT)

In this chapter, we find Jesus making a distinction between God's Word and the God of the Word. He clearly states that God's Word points directly to Him, like a roadmap into His presence. The religious leaders of His day were poring over the very Scriptures that were all about Jesus, but they couldn't recognize Him standing in their midst. This clearly proves that there's a big difference between knowing about someone theoretically and knowing that individual personally!

I once spoke at a church in Raleigh, North Carolina. It was my first time traveling to the Tar Heel State, and I was really excited. I'm a fan of the University of North Carolina (UNC) men's basketball program, and their facility is located in Chapel Hill, not too far from where I'd be ministering.

On my day off in Raleigh, my driver, Isaiah, took me out for the day and my only request was to visit the campus of UNC. Arriving there, we immediately went to the Dean E. Smith Center. As we circled around the facility, I became giddy. Inside, there were many team photos, but the ones that captivated me most were from the 1981 to 1984 seasons, the years Michael Jordan was on the team.

After a few minutes, I looked at Isaiah and said, "Bro, little did Jordan know that in the years ahead, he'd win six championships, become a six-time finals MVP, five-time NBA MVP, ten-time scoring champion, fourteen-time NBA All-Star, be selected for eleven all-NBA teams, and . . ." On and on I went, listing Jordan's accomplishments and monumental moments throughout his illustrious career. And this was before the *Last Dance* documentary!

Isaiah was amazed at how much I knew about Michael Jordan. But then it dawned on me that I would know so much about a person who I've never met. To be honest, it felt kind of creepy. I'm surprised I wasn't wearing Air Jordans—then I would've *really* felt obsessive!

Sadly, many believers are like this with God. They know a lot about His personal qualities and many great accomplishments, but don't know Him personally. They can recite Bible verses and tell about the miracles, but they have no personal stories to share. They're content reading about Him in their Bible or downloading the latest podcast, yet they fail to experience the Lord for themselves. In regard to this, A.W. Tozer wrote:

> Why do some persons "find" God in a way that others do not? Why does God manifest His Presence to some and let multitudes of others struggle along in the half-light of imperfect Christian experience? Of course, the will of God is the same for all. He has no favorites within His household. All He has ever done for any of His children He will do for all of His children. The difference lies not with God but with us.[2]

The difference lies not with God, but with us. We are as close to God as we choose to be.

Job, after conversations with his friends who thought they knew a lot about God, found himself having an encounter with God that shifted everything. Afterward, what Job thought he knew about God was nothing compared to personally experiencing God:

> "I admit I once lived by rumors of you; now I have it all firsthand—from my own eyes and ears! I'm sorry—forgive me. I'll

never do that again, I promise! I'll never again live on crusts of hearsay, crumbs of rumor." (Job 42:5 MSG)

Like Job, are you living off rumors and hearsay about God? Have you experienced God firsthand for yourself? If not, be encouraged! Look what Jesus Himself promised to those who love Him:

> "The person who has My commands and keeps them is the one who [really] loves Me; and whoever [really] loves Me will be loved by My Father, and I [too] will love him and will show (reveal, manifest) Myself to him. [I will let Myself be clearly seen by him and make Myself real to him.]" (John 14:21 AMPC)

Wow! What a promise! Jesus desires to make Himself real to you! Just like the encounter I shared with you, you too can experience the Lord in a profound way. Although we cannot determine how He will reveal Himself to us, we are assured that He will. Therefore, finding God is not a matter of distance; it's a matter of experience.

The Bible speaks of two types of the presence of God: His *omnipresence* and His *manifest presence*. God's *omnipresence* simply means that God is everywhere at all times, whether we are aware of it or not. David referred to this when he wrote:

> If I ascend into heaven, You are there; if I make my bed in hell, behold, You are there. If I take the wings of the morning, and dwell in the uttermost parts of the sea, even there Your hand shall lead me, and Your right hand shall hold me. (Psalm 139:8–10)

There's not a place where God isn't.

God's *manifest presence* is when His presence becomes real and undeniable! The word "manifest" means "readily perceived by the senses; easily understood or recognized by the mind." This is what Jesus promises in John 14:21 and that's what every God-chaser desires to have! It's these very encounters that will take us higher, shifting us from knowing the Lord as a concept to knowing Him through personal experience.

Keep drawing close to God, and He will draw closer to you.

## Shift from Theory to Revelation

Shortly after my dramatic encounter with God's Spirit, God began to open up to me revelation from Scripture in a greater degree. During that time, He gave me a vision that unlocked the truths I'm about to share.

In the vision, I saw a large table set with a beautiful white tablecloth and three plates—two of them were full of food. The third plate, from which I was eating, was only half full of food. I wasn't sure what type of food this was, but I was enjoying the meal, gobbling food down like I'd just come off a forty-day fast!

While I was eating, my eyes caught sight of the second plate of food. This made me super curious, so I stopped eating from my plate and moved to the second. Once I arrived at the second plate, I noticed the third plate and couldn't contain my excitement. Before I could run to the third plate, though, I heard a loud voice declare, "Stop! Go back and finish your first plate, then move on to the second and third."

Here's the lesson that the Lord began to reveal to me: First, there's an abundance of revelation to feed on. Jesus once shared, "To you it has been given to know the mystery of the kingdom of God; but to those who are outside, all things come in parables" (Mark 4:11).

In this verse, Jesus differentiates between two groups of people: those who *are in* the kingdom of God, and those who *are outside* of the kingdom of God. Those who are outside do not have the right to know the mysteries of the kingdom. However, as believers, we are no longer strangers and foreigners, but fellow citizens with the saints and members of the household of God. Therefore, we have legal access to the realm of revelation. The hidden things are reserved for us to feed on. They are ours by inheritance.

Now, don't let the word "mystery" confuse you. A mystery is simply that which is unexplained, untold, or unknown. Think *secrets* and *hidden truths*. Jesus desires to reveal to us the mysteries, secrets, and hidden truths of His kingdom. He yearns to explain the unexplained, to tell the untold, and to make known the unknown.

It's time for us to get out of the shallow and into the deeper things of God. It's time to access new levels of revelation. Heaven has what we want—the answers and solutions we're looking for. There is revelation reserved in heaven specifically for our generation. There are mysteries and secrets of the Lord that have been shut up until now. They have been concealed from past generations and are now being released so that we can effectively release God's kingdom here on earth.

What might that mean? I believe there are . . .

- medical breakthroughs yet to be discovered.
- songs and books yet to be written.
- technological advancements yet to be invented.
- designs that can reshape the quality and efficiency of how we do life.

The list is endless.

In regard to our day, the prophet Daniel was informed by the Angel Gabriel:

> But you, O Daniel, shut up the words and seal the Book until the time of the end. [Then] many shall run to and fro *and* search anxiously [through the Book], and knowledge [of God's purposes as revealed by His prophets] shall be increased *and* become great. (Daniel 12:4 AMPC)

According to Scripture and prophecy, the last days will be marked by an increase of knowledge. It doesn't take a genius to realize that we're living in the last days—also referred to as the Information Age. Just think back on the past few decades, and it becomes evident that we've experienced an increase of knowledge, especially in the areas of science, medicine, and technology. Even how we access this increase of knowledge has dramatically changed with the advancement of technological devices and the invention of the World Wide Web and artificial intelligence.

Although this information is now at our fingertips (or even voice activation), the Lord will only reveal certain additional things through revelation. Revelation is God making known to us what we do not know or could not have known through our natural senses. In regard to this, Jesus taught:

> [Things are hidden temporarily only as a means to revelation].
> For there is nothing hidden except to be revealed, nor is anything [temporarily] kept secret except in order that it may be made known. (Mark 4:22 AMPC)

Notice that the things Jesus wants to reveal are hidden temporarily. This explains the whole nature and function of revelation—it simply uncovers what already exists in heaven but is not known on earth. Revelation simply implies lifting the veil, much like what the late Steve Jobs would do during the 2000s whenever a new Apple product was revealed. The unveiling of the new product didn't create anything; it simply created awareness of it. Therefore, revelation is not learned—it's revealed.

One of humanity's most brilliant minds, Albert Einstein, admitted, "I came upon none of my discoveries through the process of rational thinking."[3] His ideas were divinely inspired.

In a similar way, Larry Page, the cofounder of Google, was only a twenty-two-year-old graduate student when he divinely received the blueprint for what would become the Google search engine. During a dream, Larry saw the world's information in an entirely new way. He perceived how all the information on the internet could be gathered systematically according to rank and relevance. Once he woke up, he spent two hours scribbling down an algorithm that eventually revolutionized the way we access information.[4]

There's so much to be revealed! My heart feels like exploding every time I think about it! When we grasp these truths, the way we view our relationship with God is revolutionized. We become more excited to meet with Him and to receive His counsel. And this is exactly what I was alluding to in the previous chapter. God Himself encourages us:

> "Call to Me and I will answer you, and tell you [and even show you] great and mighty things, [things which have been confined and hidden], which you do not know *and* understand *and* cannot distinguish." (Jeremiah 33:3 AMP)

This type of knowledge sheds fresh perspective on Paul's words of "eye has not seen, nor ear heard, nor have entered into the heart of man the things which God has prepared for those who love Him" (1 Corinthians 2:9), but we *can know* these things by His Spirit!

And here's what we must understand: We can't know everything, but we can know those things that pertain to our area of calling and influence. For instance, if you're a surgeon, you can access revelation for a new way of operating on particular injuries or diseases that hasn't been known before. The possibilities are limitless and apply to all sectors of knowledge.

Here are some other lessons the Lord taught me from the vision I received. We've seen how Jesus wants to reveal His mysteries, secrets, and hidden truths to us through revelation. After giving insights of such knowledge, Jesus taught on how we can feed our spirit and mind with what the Lord speaks to us:

> Be careful what you are hearing. The measure [of thought and study] you give [to the truth you hear] will be the measure [of virtue and knowledge] that comes back to you—and more [besides] will be given to you who hear. (Mark 4:24 AMPC)

Once God speaks to you, what is the measure of "thought and study" you give to what He revealed? The way you steward revelation will determine whether you'll receive new levels of it or not. The process of thought and study referred to here is what the Bible calls *meditation*. Many become uncomfortable at the mention of this word because of its association with New Age and Buddhist practices. However, biblical meditation differs from Eastern religions in that biblical meditation is not the emptying of the mind, but rather the filling of the mind with God's Word.

The practice of meditation allows an idea or concept to mature and develop. While we're contemplating, studying, and diving deeper into what has been revealed to us, we'll receive greater clarity of meaning.

After I received the vision of the three plates, I kept pondering what God had revealed. As I did, greater clarity came to me. I began to see certain verses and passages of the Bible in a new way. Things I'd skimmed over before became a gold mine for me to dig into. And now I'm writing this book about them! When we invest quality thought and study into what is revealed to us, we'll receive greater levels of revelation.

When Larry Page awoke from his dream, his immediate response was to write it down. This allowed the idea to progress from his mind to his notepad. Page's mind was then free to receive greater clarity to the initial idea. But what if Larry had brushed off his dream, concluding that he'd maybe eaten too much pizza the night before? What a loss that would've been!

*Meditation is the digestive system of the soul. It allows us to assimilate and absorb all that God speaks to us.*

In Ezekiel 2 and 3, the Lord literally gives Ezekiel a scroll to eat! His exact words were, "'Son of man, eat what I am giving you—eat this scroll! Then go and give its message to the people of Israel'" (Ezekiel 3:1 NLT). It's interesting that before this encounter, Ezekiel was not yet a prophetic voice to Israel. It wasn't until after Ezekiel had fully assimilated all that God had given him, that he was commissioned to prophesy. We read that he's told by the Lord:

"Son of man, let all my words sink deep into your own heart first. Listen to them carefully for yourself. Then go to your people in exile and say to them, 'This is what the Sovereign LORD says!' Do this whether they listen to you or not." (Ezekiel 3:10–11 NLT)

The way in which God's words sunk deeply into Ezekiel's heart as he ate them occurred through meditation. When we meditate, we feed ourselves, so in turn, we can feed others.

When you give revelation the respect it deserves, it will reward you. This communicates to God that you value what He reveals. And when you value what He shares, He'll trust you with more.

Consider these words by Charles Spurgeon: "Let me compare meditation to a wine press. By reading and research and study we gather the grapes; but it is by meditation we press out the juices of those grapes and obtain the wine."

There is revelation reserved in heaven for you. Don't wait any longer. Make the shift from theory to revelation.

## The Shift from Servant to Friend

Everything I've shared in this chapter means nothing unless it's done within an intimate friendship. That's the motivation behind Jesus making Himself known in personal experience and sharing the secrets of His heart. Understand, He's passionate about His relationship with you! For us to engage in this intimate relationship, we'll need to shift from the mindset of servants to that of friends. Hear what Jesus shared:

> "I have never called you 'servants,' because a master doesn't confide in his servants, and servants don't always understand what the master is doing. But I call you my most intimate friends, for I reveal to you everything that I've heard from my Father." (John 15:15 TPT)

The most obvious distinction between a servant and a friend is the level of relationship experienced. Friends have the privilege of gaining inside information. I've heard it said that servants work for favor, while friends work from a place of favor.

Abraham was known as a friend of God, and the Lord kept him in the loop about what He was doing. When the Lord was ready to deal with Sodom and Gomorrah, He said, "Shall I hide from Abraham what I am doing . . ." (Genesis 18:17).

Moses was also a friend of God, and he too was kept in the loop about what the Lord was doing. God "made known His ways to Moses, His acts to the children of Israel" (Psalm 103:7). Moses not only saw what God did, he also knew why He was doing it.

Jesus, too, modeled the type of relationship we can have with God and gave us insight into His relationship with the Father:

> "Every day my Father is at work, and I will be too!" . . . So Jesus said, 'I speak to you timeless truth. The Son is not able to do anything from himself or through my own initiative. I only do the works that I see the Father doing, for the Son does the same works as his Father. Because the Father loves his Son so much, he always reveals to me everything that he is about to do. And you will all be amazed when he shows me even greater works than what you've seen so far!" (John 5:17, 19–20 TPT)

Jesus was in constant contact with His Father. Because Jesus prioritized His relationship with God, He was consistently in the know and only did what He saw His Father doing. This type of relationship is available to you and me!

---

On a particular day, Jesus and His disciples entered a village in which two sisters named Mary and Martha lived. Martha invited Jesus and His followers to have a meal at her home. After traveling through several towns on a productive ministry trip, the opportunity to have a home-cooked meal and rest was a good idea.

Once at the house, Jesus had everyone's attention—except Martha, who was busy tending to her guests. Mary was among those listening attentively to Jesus. This greatly annoyed Martha, so much so that she interrupted Jesus and vented, "Lord, don't You think it's unfair that my sister left me to do all the work by myself? You should tell her to get up and help me!"

Martha had a point. I, too, would be annoyed if my sister weren't helping. However, Jesus didn't seem bothered that His food might be delayed—although I'm sure Peter's stomach was growling, and he was ready to side with Martha. The Lord answered her:

> "Martha, my beloved Martha. Why are you upset and troubled, pulled away by all these many distractions? Are they really that important? Mary has discovered the one thing most important by choosing to sit at my feet. She is undistracted, and I won't take this privilege from her." (Luke 10:41–42 TPT)

Initially, Jesus's response probably added to Martha's frustration. Still, Jesus wasn't pushing her away—He was trying to pull her closer. Martha's serving and busyness was the wall separating her from what Mary was experiencing. Jesus wanted Martha to realize what was most important, which was listening to Him speak.

Secrets are reserved for close companions who, like Mary, are willing to come aside from their busyness and invest quality time to grow closer to Jesus. Most of us disclose our deepest and most intimate thoughts and feelings to trusted friends. The Lord is no different. God has secrets, and He is looking for some friends to share them with. It is an open invitation to all those who desire friendship with Him.

David, known as a man after God's heart, revealed, "There's a private place reserved for the devoted lovers of Yahweh, where they sit near him and receive the revelation-secrets of his promises" (Psalm 25:14 TPT).

The private place David spoke of is God's presence. It's in that intimate place that God's secrets are made known. Just like Jesus shared, God is working, and He wants to partner with you. The Lord has plans for you, and He wants you to know what they are. Jeremiah posed the question: "For who among them has stood in the council of the LORD to see and to hear his word, or who has paid attention to his word and listened?" (Jeremiah 23:18 ESV).

In his book *The Lost Art of Practicing His Presence*, James W. Goll shares that the Hebrew word for "council" in this verse is *cowd*, which means "a session" or "a company of persons in close deliberation." This word implies intimacy, as in secret consultation. And by comparison, our English word "council" also refers to a group of people called together for discussion or advice. Just as there are earthly councils of men and women who come together to discuss and advise the best plan of action for their respective spheres of influence, there is also a council that takes place in heaven, presided over by God Almighty, where we can hear and receive the counsel and secrets of the Lord.

That's why we're personally invited to come up higher, so we can join the conversation and enter God's "hearing room" and listen to the deliberation of His council. By doing so, we'll take part in what God is doing on the earth. As co-laborers with Him, we have a significant role in bringing heaven's rule and reality to our world. All this begins by walking closely with God—listening to and obeying His voice.

It's time you shift from being a mere servant to being an intimate friend.

### Draw Near

If you've made it this far through this chapter without stopping to pray, then I encourage you now to spend time with the Lord. Allow these truths you've read to become real to you. Each of us are as close to God as we have chosen to be. But we don't have to stay at our current level. We can live from higher places.

There's more, and it's available to you. You can shift from hearsay to personal experience, from theory to revelation, and from a servant to a friend. Let's level up in our relationship with God.

## CHEAT CODE

### Remember
- Knowing God in theory is not the same as knowing Him personally.
- Jesus deeply desires to make Himself real to us.
- Through revelation, God makes known what cannot be known through our natural senses.
- Meditation for the Christian is the "filling of the self with God's Word."
- Jesus longs for us to be His friend, not merely a servant.

### Reflect
1. What instances do you recall where God was most real to you?
2. What might you do to deepen your friendship with Jesus?

# 5

# DOORS, WINDOWS, AND OPPORTUNITY

*A Sudden Good Break Can Change Everything!*

Advancing to new levels usually occurs through the gateway of opportunity, which opens a pathway to new rooms and playing fields. Life is full of these opportunities—life-defining moments orchestrated by God as He works out His divine plan for our life. Moments that can forever change the trajectory of them.

Toward the close of 2004, my brother, Jay, and I were driving to the beach with our friend, Jonathan. I was in the back seat; the others were up front. During the drive to Sydney's beautiful northern beaches, Jono (Aussie slang for Jonathan) slipped a CD into the player from a sermon series by John Bevere.

"Boys!" Jono shouted. "You have to listen to this guy. He just spoke at Hillsong Church last weekend. He's amazing!"

During the hour-long drive, we listened to John Bevere, who was unlike the preachers I was used to hearing. He spoke with passion and conviction—I was glued to every word! I sat there crying, absorbing the message like a sponge. John was sharing things I had never heard before. When the message ended, I heard these words in my heart: "You're going to know John, and you're going to work for him!"

Although I had no idea what John Bevere looked like or where he was from, I felt a connection to him. Something in my spirit also knew that my future was somehow connected to him. This began to make more sense in the months and years that followed.

Two weeks later, I learned that John had a ministry office in Sydney. Once a week, I would visit and help around the office with small tasks. Over time, I became acquainted with John's Australian staff and established a strong friendship with the team members.

Early the following year, I met John Bevere in person at a conference while he was speaking in our nation's capital, Canberra. I drove three hours south of Sydney to attend the meetings and to serve at the book table. To say I was excited would be an understatement. After the first service, Esther, the office manager, called me over so that she could introduce me to John.

"John, I'd like you to meet Chris Pace," Esther said. "He's a good friend of ours!"

"Hey, Chris, nice to meet you!" John said, extending his hand. I shook his hand and did not say a word. It wasn't that I had nothing to say; I just couldn't speak. Something unusual occurred the moment our hands touched, and I was lost for words. I felt a warm, liquid feeling ooze through my arm and permeate my entire body. I must have stood for a minute staring at my arm, still speechless. John had a confused look on his face! After the awkward silence, Esther motioned me toward the book table. But, despite the embarrassment, I knew something special had taken place.

Fast forward five years, and I had become an employee at Messenger International, the ministry led by John Bevere, even making two trips to Messenger's headquarters in Colorado Springs. During those years, I had developed strong friendships with the team in the U.S., and there were talks of transferring me to America. All along, I was believing for the opportunity to move to the U.S. and join the team in Colorado. Messenger's office in Australia had closed at the end of 2010, so the potential of this move seemed more possible.

Early in 2011, I received a phone call from the ministry's CFO, and he offered me the opportunity to work for John and Lisa Bevere in Colorado. He told me to take a day to pray about it, but I already knew what my answer would be. Although it felt like fireworks were exploding in my heart, and I wanted to instantly accept his offer, I agreed to pray.

As a side note, what made this moment even more special was that God had given me a prophetic word for the year ahead. The word I'd received for 2011 was "opportunity." The Holy Spirit had said to me, "This will be a year of opportunity. You won't have to look for opportunity; opportunity will find you."

When I got off the phone, I immediately thought of what God's Spirit had said to me. While I prayed, however, I sensed an uneasiness in my spirit. I immediately thought I was just being fearful. I tried to pray through it, but the feeling intensified. I was puzzled—*all the years of believing God for this opportunity, and now is God saying no?* I was confused and quickly becoming angry.

About an hour later, once I had quieted myself, I heard the Holy Spirit firmly instruct me to remain in Australia. I still sensed I was to one day move to America and work with the Beveres, but it wasn't the right time. I strongly sensed that I was to stay and commit myself to serving at my local church.

I knew I had heard from God, so the next day—reluctantly—I turned down the opportunity.

My church was part of one of the largest churches both in Australia and around the world. For the next seven months, I faithfully served at my church's youth ministry. Although I knew I was obeying God, I still struggled with discouragement. At times, I even questioned if I had heard from God and made the right decision.

One morning while I was exercising at the gym, I received a call from my campus pastor. I don't normally take calls during a cardio session, but I knew I had to answer this one. She'd called to inform me that the church needed someone to do the live Sunday announcements, which were played on the screens at all the church campuses around Sydney. If I accepted, it would require me to go into the church studio to be filmed making the announcements once a month.

Initially, I hesitated, thinking, *What if I'm terrible? What if I look stupid on the big screens? What if people poke fun at me?* All sorts of negative thoughts bombarded my mind. I wasn't used to being in front of people—whether in person or on screen. Before I could think any further, though, I responded, "I'll do it!"

For the following months, I recorded and announced the church news. During that time, the Lord spoke to our senior pastor about me. While he watched me on screen, he began to recognize the call of God on my life to preach. At leaders' meetings, he would openly share his thoughts about me with the other lead pastors. (I know this because my campus pastor shared it with me.) Within two months, I was commissioned to preach in the church's main services.

On November 27, 2011, I preached my first sermon. It was the first of many, and more opportunities to preach opened for me. I also became involved with leading youth and young adults' ministries for our campus.

Looking back to the start of 2011, and the way in which I'd turned down—until then—the biggest opportunity of my life, I could see the wisdom of God through it all. The years after that were pivotal for my growth and development. I had been given a taste of what I was called and gifted to do.

## The Game-Changer

Opportunity is the doorway to destiny, and once opportunity is seized, a whole new season will open up to us. With this in mind, let's discuss the concept of opportunity by beginning with these wise words from Solomon:

I have observed something else under the sun. The fastest runner doesn't always win the race, and the strongest warrior doesn't always win the battle. The wise sometimes go hungry, and the skillful are not necessarily wealthy. And those who are educated don't always lead successful lives. It is all decided by *chance*, by being in the right place at the right time. (Ecclesiastes 9:11 NLT)

In regard to success, Solomon revealed, "it is all decided by *chance*." The word "chance" is an interesting word, which when you hear it, you probably think "fate" or "luck." Although these are key factors, at its core, the word "chance" means "opportunity." Therefore, we can conclude that the successful person is the one who recognizes and seizes opportunity.

As Solomon stated, success doesn't always come to those who are the most gifted and talented (although they may have better chances); rather, it comes to those who take their chances—who seize opportunity!

This is where the God factor enters the picture. The Lord declared through the prophet Jeremiah, "I know what I'm doing. I have it all planned out—plans to take care of you, not abandon you, plans to give you the future you hope for" (Jeremiah 29:11 MSG). God's plans for us include moments of favor and opportunity. As we follow His leading for our life, we'll find ourselves stepping into these moments. Moments we couldn't orchestrate on our own.

Through Isaiah, the Lord assured, "I'll go ahead of you, clearing and paving the road. I'll break down bronze city gates, smash padlocks, kick down barred entrances" (Isaiah 45:2 MSG). If we're obedient, nothing can stop God's plans from coming to pass. Be assured, God can make a way for you where there seems no way. If needed, He'll remove all stops—breaking bronze city gates, smashing padlocks, kicking down barred entrances and, yes, even parting seas!

It's amazing the places you'll find yourself when God is on your side. You'll be left wondering, *How did I get here?* It was God all along!

When God is for you, no one and nothing can be against you. This is why David could let go and express, "'I am trusting You, O LORD, saying, 'You are my God! My future is in your hands'" (Psalm 31:14-15 NLT).

## Seizing Opportunity

Opportunity can come unexpectedly, and as the Proverb says, "a sudden good break can turn life around" (Proverbs 13:12 MSG). For this reason, it is important that we are prepared, positioned, and perceiving for opportunity.

### *Prepared for Opportunity*

Opportunity rarely comes at a moment of our choosing. Therefore, we must be ready, whether the time is favorable or not. Let's face it, we may not know when our moments of opportunity may come, but we can surely prepare ourselves for their arrival. If you have prepared for something, you'll recognize it when it appears. Ralph Waldo Emerson penned, "People only see what they are prepared to see."

Before my first preaching opportunity, I had been preparing myself in private. During my times of prayer, I would receive ideas for sermons. I knew I was called to preach, but at the time I didn't have any opportunity to do so. While serving in our youth ministry, I sensed I needed to be ready to preach. On weekends, I'd often spend several hours studying God's Word and putting messages together. It was so much fun! Even though I had no speaking opportunities, I prepared as if I did. And I'm glad I did, because when the opportunity to preach came later that year, I was ready. I had developed the spiritual and intellectual muscles to step into that moment.

If you're always waiting for opportunity to present itself before you begin preparing yourself, you could miss your moment. Zig Ziglar taught, "Success occurs when preparation meets opportunity."

How can you start preparing yourself for what God has planned for you?

*Positioned for Opportunity*
Let's return to Solomon's words about opportunity: "It is all decided by chance, by being in *the right place* at the right time" (Ecclesiastes 9:11 NLT). Opportunity is always linked to the right place. The right place will attract the right opportunities.

Ted Williams (not the legendary baseball Hall of Famer) is known as the man with the golden voice. His story has always been a source of encouragement for me. As a young man, Ted had a promising career as a radio announcer. However, due to drug and alcohol addiction, he found himself broke and living on the streets. At the age of fifty-three, after seventeen years of living on the streets, Ted decided he'd had enough and wanted to get his life together again.

In 2010, hoping for a better future, Ted stood along Interstate 71 in Columbus, Ohio, holding a sign that read: "I have a God-given gift of voice. I'm an ex-radio announcer who has fallen on hard times." That morning, a videographer from the *Columbus Dispatch* happened to drive by and was intrigued by Ted's sign. Curious, the videographer pulled alongside Ted and asked him for a demonstration of his radio voice. As Ted gave him a sample, the videographer recorded him on his iPhone.

Later that day, as the videographer returned to his office, he posted the video of Ted on the *Columbus Dispatch* website. Unexpectedly, the video went viral, accumulating over 12 million views on YouTube. In a series of events, this earned Ted an interview with a local radio station, which provided him the opportunity to share his story and his desire to get his life back on track.

From there, Ted's gift began to offer opportunities for him again. Job offers poured in from all over the country, including Ohio's local NBA team, the Cleveland Cavaliers. Ted also appeared on *The Today Show*.

Ted put his life back together. Now he travels the country sharing motivational speeches while raising awareness of the dangers of drug and alcohol abuse. He has also written a book and uses the proceeds to support the homeless community in the Columbus, Ohio, area. What I love about Ted's story is that it shows that no matter how far off-track you may have drifted, it is not too late to begin again. There is always hope. And that's the power of opportunity. Ted was in the right place, at the right time.

Proper placement is one of God's primary purposes for our life. God made places before He made people. The right place includes the right city, state, and country. It could be the right church or the right school, because location is very important when it comes to opportunity. When I chose to obey God and remain in Australia, the right opportunities for me in that season of my life presented themselves.

Interestingly, the right place doesn't always feel like the right place, as was true for me at first. But you can be sure the dots will eventually connect.

### Perceiving Opportunity

When it comes to opportunity, timing is everything. Once again, let's hear what Solomon has to say on the topic:

> "It is all decided by chance, by being in the right place at *the right time*" (Ecclesiastes 9:11 NLT).

We've looked at the importance of being prepared and positioned for opportunity; now it's time to look at the need to perceive it. This has to do with timing. Solomon also wrote, "There's an *opportune time* to do things, *a right time* for everything on the earth" (Ecclesiastes 3:1 MSG).

In the ancient Greek rendering of the Bible, there were two distinct words used for time: *chronos* and *kairos*. *Chronos* refers to the duration of time, such as minutes and hours, days and weeks, months and years. *Kairos*, on the other hand, refers to an appointed time or the right time. Therefore, *chronos* is more quantitative, whereas *kairos* is more qualitative. *Kairos* often includes the idea of an opportunity or suitable time for an action to take place. When discerning God's timing in relation to opportunity, we are referring to *kairos*—an opportune and appointed time.

This reminds me of a situation that occurred in 1 Kings 19 where Elijah was sent to Gilgal to anoint Elisha as prophet in his place. When Elijah arrived on the scene, he found Elisha plowing the fields with his oxen. As he got close enough to him, Elijah threw his mantle upon Elisha, signifying the call to become his successor.

Elisha understood very well what had taken place but first wanted to say goodbye to his parents. To ensure he didn't miss his moment, Elijah warned, "Go on back, but think about what I have done to you" (1 Kings 19:20 NLT). Take note of his statement, "Think about what I have done to you." In other words, "Don't miss your moment of opportunity. Your response to what has just taken place is pivotal for the fulfillment of God's plan for your life." Elijah was emphasizing the importance of recognizing the seriousness and significance of the moment.

Rarely do we get to know, in the moment, the impact of that moment. That's why we're required to perceive it. Windows of opportunity don't always remain open forever. In the words of Leonard Ravenhill, "The opportunity of a lifetime needs to be seized during the lifetime of the opportunity."

When God is doing a new thing in our life, He expects us to discern what He's doing and respond. He says through Isaiah:

> "I am doing something brand new, *something unheard of*. Even now it sprouts and grows and matures. *Don't you perceive it?* I will make a way in the wilderness and open up flowing streams in the desert." (Isaiah 43:19 TPT)

What we need to grasp is that these appointed times can propel us further into our God-given destiny—just like Elisha seizing his opportunity propelled him further into his destiny. I'm sure that when he made the decision, he had a lot of questions. But he also trusted that things would become clearer as he stepped out in faith.

As an example, look at Abraham, our father of faith:

> Faith motivated Abraham to obey God's call and leave the familiar to discover the territory he was destined to inherit from God. So he left with only a promise and without even knowing ahead of time where he was going, Abraham stepped out in faith. (Hebrews 11:8 TPT)

In times like these, you don't have to see the whole staircase; you just have to take the first step. Abraham stepped out in faith, not knowing ahead of time where he was going.

Here are three things to keep in mind when discerning opportunity: *First, the right time may not always feel right.* Drawing from Solomon's well of wisdom once again, "He who observes the wind [and waits for all conditions to be favorable] will not sow, and he who regards the clouds will not reap" (Ecclesiastes 11:4 AMPC).

If you are waiting for the perfect time before you take action, you will be waiting for a long time. The right time doesn't always mean perfect conditions. When you have this mindset, you'll often find an excuse for why it is not a good time to act . . . and talk yourself out of it.

*Second, let peace act as an umpire.* Paul wrote, "And let the peace (soul harmony which comes) from Christ rule (act as umpire continually) in your hearts [deciding and settling with finality all questions that arise in your minds, in that peaceful state]" (Colossians 3:15 AMPC).

Umpires direct the flow of a game. They determine what's acceptable play or not. Likewise, let peace determine the way you engage life. When I turned down the opportunity in 2011, it was because I lacked peace. It didn't feel right. I'm glad I paid attention to that, rather than forcing my own way.

*Third, let God direct your steps.* He does this not by pushing us around, but by His Spirit gently working within us, prompting us to do what pleases Him. As Jesus instructed, "And He said to them, Come after Me [as disciples—*letting Me be your Guide*], *follow* Me, and I will make you fishers of men! At once they left their nets and became His disciples [sided with His party and *followed* Him]" (Matthew 4:19–20 AMPC). Following Jesus requires that you allow Him to be your guide.

There are many benefits to having a travel guide. These benefits include saving you time, as the guide thinks ahead and plans the journey for you. Guides know where to go and what to avoid. They can even give you VIP access to significant places.

In April 2015, I visited Disneyland. I had dreamed of going to Disneyland ever since I was a little boy, and it was my first time there. I met up with a friend, Aly, who was an employee at Disneyland and had volunteered to spend the day as my tour guide. She knew the place back to front and inside out. Therefore, not only did she save me time and planning, and a possible headache, but she also provided for me an experience money couldn't buy. Her enthusiasm for all the rides, attractions, and characters made me appreciate my visit so much more. Aly also gave me quick access to rides that I would have had to wait hours for while standing in line. This is the nature of a travel guide.

As you follow the Lord, and the ultimate guide living in you—the Holy Spirit—you're in for the time of your life!

In C.S. Lewis's Narnia book, *Prince Caspian*, he captures the importance of allowing God to lead. In chapter nine, Lucy, Susan, Peter, and Edmund, along with a strange character named Trumpkin, find themselves lost in the woods of Narnia. To make matters worse, they're attacked by a bear that Trumpkin manages to kill. Next, they come to an edge of a gorge overlooking a landscape that they fail to recognize. As they are all feeling helpless and lost, Lucy suddenly sees a vision of Aslan in the distance. Deep down, she senses that Aslan wants them to follow him. Excitedly, Lucy shares her vision with everyone.

However, her excitement is not mutual. A dispute breaks out as Peter and Susan have doubts about Lucy's apparent sighting of Aslan. Undeterred, Lucy stands her ground, confident that Aslan is showing them the way. The only explanation she can give is that she just "knew." A vote is taken, and they all decide to go the opposite direction from where Lucy was certain Aslan was leading them.

As the story unfolds, they end up experiencing a challenging and awful day, because they "leaned on their own understanding" and ignored Aslan's leading.

Likewise, there are many times the Lord is leading you a certain way; yet, if you choose to ignore His promptings and guidance, you could find yourself veering off the path He's planned for you. For this reason, the Scriptures tell us:

> Trust GOD from the bottom of your heart; don't try to figure out everything on your own. Listen for GOD's voice in everything you do, everywhere you go; he's the one who will keep you on track.
> (Proverbs 3:5–6 MSG)

Learning to perceive opportunity is learning to listen for God's voice in everything you do and everywhere you go. As you do, the Lord is the One who will keep you on track.

### Go for a Test-Drive

Seizing an opportunity doesn't always mean huge, irreversible changes! I think people often are afraid to make decisions because they're scared to overcommit. But opportunity gives us exposure to new places, things, and people. Having exposure to new facts, ideas, and cultures broadens our thinking and perspective. With this exposure, we're allowed to gain new insights and information. Afterward, we can evaluate our experiences and even adjust decisions.

As a side note, if you're the biggest fish in the pond, perhaps it's time to find a lake or even an ocean. If we only remain exposed to the familiar things we've become accustomed to, we'll stop growing. Don't allow feelings of inadequacy or inferiority to stop you from exploring new ways of doing things. Make room for yourself to stretch and grow.

In his book *Destiny*, T.D. Jakes offers a fresh perspective on the importance of exposure:

> Gaining exposure is like a test-drive on a car. You enter a new arena and see if it fits. You see what it costs you to be in that environment and determine whether you want to pay the price. You make inquiries in your new environment, just like you would about the car, and find out all that you can. You have to work your way into the feel of what God is exposing you to, just like you work your way into the feel of a new car. You ask yourself, "Does this lifestyle fit me?" When it doesn't fit your needs or your self-image, you know to keep looking.[5]

View opportunity as a test-drive. Get a feel and gain experience in the field you've entered. Perhaps you'll realize it's not what you thought it was going to be, and you can change your mind. That's okay! Maybe you thought you wanted to be a counselor, but you couldn't keep your mouth shut. Then you realized that becoming a teacher or coach is more suited for you. Exposure offers the experience to explore and evaluate so that we can make more informed decisions.

Today, we have a variety of ways to gain exposure and experience. In times past, people had to travel for days or months to gain exposure and have the opportunity to explore new things. In the Old Testament, the queen of Sheba traveled a great distance so she could gain exposure to the wisdom of Solomon:

> When the queen of Sheba experienced for herself Solomon's wisdom and saw with her own eyes the palace he had built, the meals that were served, the impressive array of court officials and sharply dressed waiters, the lavish crystal, and the elaborate worship extravagant with Whole-Burnt-Offerings at the steps leading up to The Temple of God, it took her breath away. She said to the king, "It's all true! Your reputation for accomplishment

and wisdom that reached all the way to my country is confirmed. I wouldn't have believed it if I hadn't seen it for myself; they didn't exaggerate! Such wisdom and elegance—far more than I could ever have imagined. (1 Kings 10:1–6 MSG)

Once the queen of Sheba had a taste for herself of all she had heard about Solomon and Israel, she was blown away! It was more than she expected. With her newfound exposure, she expressed:

Lucky the men and women who work for you, *getting to be around you* every day and hear your wise words firsthand! And blessed be GOD, your God, who took such a liking to you and made you king. Clearly, GOD's love for Israel is behind this, making you king to keep a just order and nurture a God-pleasing people." (1 Kings 10:8–9 MSG)

Did you capture that? "Lucky the men and women who work for you, getting to be around you every day and hear your wise words firsthand!" In other words, blessed are those who have constant exposure to your wisdom and ways. Exposure is your test-drive. Just as the queen of Sheba did, go for a test-drive and see if it's what you're looking for. Ask, seek, knock—you'll be thankful you did.

## The Risk Factor

Seizing opportunity is risky, but without facing risk you'll never bridge the gap between *what has been* and *what could be*.

Risk your life and get *more* than you ever dreamed of. Play it safe and end up holding the bag. (Luke 19:26 MSG)

Progressing to new levels will require risk. Risk always involves exposure to danger or uncertainty. An opportunity may not be dangerous, but uncertainty is present in every opportunity. Not knowing what life will be like on the other side—that's sobering. The truth is, we must be willing to fail in order to succeed. There would be no risk without the possibility of danger or uncertainty.

We see this idea played out in Numbers 13 and 14. These chapters pick up the account of the twelve spies who were commissioned to spy out the land of Canaan on behalf of the children of Israel. It was an opportune time for them to see firsthand the long-awaited Promised Land. However, as history tells it, the Israelites missed their opportunity when ten of the twelve returned with a negative report.

With the exception of Caleb and Joshua, a whole generation missed out on what God had destined for them, because they failed to perceive their moment of opportunity. They weren't willing to embrace the unknown and risks of danger. By playing it safe, they spent the rest of their lives roaming the wilderness.

Risk-takers bridge the gap between where they are and where they want to be. They are aware that the biggest risk often is taking no risk at all. I'm not encouraging carelessness or irresponsibility; rather, I'm encouraging facing your fears and stepping into the great unknown. Poet T.S. Elliot said it best: "Only those who will risk going too far can possibly find out how far one can go."

## Decisions Determine Your Destiny

Opportunity provides options. These options require us to make choices. They're like intersections where you must decide which way to turn.

As a child, I loved to read *Choose Your Own Adventure* books written by R.A. Montgomery. I enjoyed these books, not only because they were addictive, but because they empowered me in a way that other books did not. At key plot points, the books allowed the reader to make decisions that actually changed the course of the story.

With every book, the author warned:

This book is different from other books. You and you alone are in charge of what happens in this story. There are dangers, choices, adventures, and consequences. You must use all of your numerous talents and much of your enormous intelligence. The wrong decision could end in disaster—even death. But, don't despair. At any time, you can go back and make another choice, alter the path of your story, and change its result.[6]

God, the author of your story, has empowered you to make choices that will shape your destiny. Perhaps you may even regret some past choices. Although you cannot turn the pages and go back, you can begin again and make choices today that will positively influence your future. You can choose to realign yourself with God's plan and purpose for your life.

In your moments of decision, your future is paved. Be prepared. Be positioned. Then perceive your moment and step into a new level of destiny—shifting from where you have potential to where you are potent.

## CHEAT CODE

### Remember
- When opportunity is seized, a whole new season opens.
- Opportunity often comes when it's least expected.
- When God is for you, no one and nothing can be against you.
- Even if you go off track, God will help you start again.
- Windows of opportunity don't stay open forever.

### Reflect
1. What opportunities in your lifetime have you seized? What opportunities did you miss? What difference has it made?
2. What opportunity is facing you now? Are you overly concerned about the risks? Is there a "test-drive" you should take to move forward?

# 6

# REPOSITION YOURSELF

*When Things Have Changed, So Must You!*

The year 2014 certainly was a game-changer for me. That's the year I migrated from Australia to America. As long as I could remember, I'd always sensed that one day I'd live in America. Then, as I mentioned in the last chapter, when the opportunity came . . . I turned it down.

Well, after a series of uniquely orchestrated events, the opportunity presented itself again. But this time, not only was the situation different, it was also the right time. So, when it came time to decide if I wanted to migrate to America and leave Australia, it was an easy decision. But, although the choice was easy, the change wasn't.

Coming to America had its challenges. Not only did I change my country, but there were also many other adjustments to be made. Some were immediate; others were gradual. I had to find my bearings in a new city and culture, become acclimated to high altitude, and learn how to drive on the wrong side of the road! After all the excitement that surrounded moving and beginning a new life in America wore off, reality set in. Although I had repositioned myself externally, I had not done so internally.

Back home, I had a lot going for me that had taken years to build. I had established relationships, a well-paying job, and a local church where my ministry dreams were coming true. Leaving Australia meant leaving all this behind.

That was easier said than done. At times, I'd check up on my friends back home and see them getting opportunities at church that I knew I could've had. It seemed like life had moved on and I'd become someone my friends used to know. It took several years for me to distance myself from the dreams, goals, and ambitions in Australia.

Most of my frustrations in the early stages of my move came from anxiously attempting to fulfill those previous dreams, goals, and ambitions in America. If I'm honest, I was afraid. I often felt like a lost little boy looking for his parents in the midst of a crowd.

I needed a reset. I had made big life changes, and I had to allow myself to catch up mentally and emotionally. I'm sure I wasn't the most pleasant person to be around in those early days. If I could go back and do things differently, I'd be more intentional about making a better transition. Leveling up involves more than just a change in position—it involves a change in disposition. The first change is external; the second one is internal.

### Rite of Passage

When God takes us to a new level, both external and internal repositioning is required. This is one of the reasons why rites of passage are a popular practice—events like graduation ceremonies, inaugurations, weddings, baptisms, and bar mitzvahs. Rites of passage help mark important transitional periods in life and are designed to assist us with moving from previous roles to preparing for new ones. With this in mind, listen to what God says about embracing change:

> Do not remember the former things, or ponder the things of the past. Listen carefully, I am about to do a new thing, now it will

spring forth; will you not be aware of it? I will even put a road in the wilderness, rivers in the desert. (Isaiah 43:18–19 AMP)

Just like a rite of passage, God encourages us to let go of the past so we can embrace the new season. Letting go can be difficult. It's not easy parting from what we've known and have become comfortable with. Embracing the future can be scary. Nothing is certain, and it requires courage to step into the unknown. The new thing that we often romanticize about means embracing a new normal. It's at this point that a person usually gets cold feet and questions whether what they've always wanted is actually what they want!

Unfortunately, this is when many stop progressing. Advancing to new levels in your destiny involves adapting to change. For example, it's a given that every year you will experience a change in seasons: spring, summer, fall, and winter. Each new season involves a degree of adapting and adjusting—winter means out go your flip-flops and tank tops and in come your coats and scarves! The ability to *adapt* allows you to let go of what used to work while embracing what is working now.

Consider a space shuttle. As it launches into outer space, it must make *adjustments*. The higher the shuttle reaches, the more it has to rid itself of. At certain heights, the shuttle detaches the boosters, because at the higher altitude, what worked to supply propulsion in the beginning, is now just weight causing drag. Likewise, the higher you go with God, there will be certain people and things you'll need to detach from because they'll hold you back. This is not easy and needs to be done by the leading of the Spirit and with grace.

In relation to change, I love what James Clear wrote in *Atomic Habits*: "You should be far more concerned with your current trajectory than with your current results." What's working now may not be what's needed to go forward. So, to resist change is to resist the transient nature of life. Life keeps changing and so must you. Thankfully, God knows our nature and inclination to resist change, and He prepares us ahead of time. Jesus taught:

> "And no one puts new wine into old wineskins; or else the new wine will burst the wineskins and be spilled, and the wineskins will be ruined. But new wine must be put into new wineskins, and both are preserved. And no one, having drunk old wine, *immediately* desires *new*; for he says, 'The old is better.'" (Luke 5:37–39)

This parable reveals the nature of change. At first, change is resisted as we hold onto the "old." Yet, the consequences of rejecting change often produce negative results, "no one puts new wine into old wineskins; or else the new wine will burst the wineskins and be spilled, and the wineskins will be ruined." A person who cannot adjust to the shifts and changes of God holds onto what God *did* while resisting what He's presently *doing*. If we're not open to change and making the necessary adjustments, we won't handle well the new thing God wants for our life and the new levels He wants for us.

On the contrary, staying open to the new things God wants to do in our life has positive results. "But new wine must be put into new wineskins, and both are preserved."

What *new wineskin* is required for you to reposition yourself and to embrace your next level? Perhaps it's a new mindset, new habits, new relationships, or learning new things?

Progress is progressive. We must continue to *grow up* as we *go up*.

## Step Up, Step In

When Joshua and the children of Israel were ready to step into the Promised Land, God gave Joshua some very clear instructions that we can also apply and learn from:

> After the death of Moses, the Lord's servant, the Lord spoke to Joshua son of Nun, Moses' assistant. He said, "Moses my ser-

vant is dead. Therefore, the time has come for you to lead these people, the Israelites, across the Jordan River into the land I am giving them. I promise you what I promised Moses: 'Wherever you set foot, you will be on land I have given you—" (Joshua 1:1–3 NLT)

The first thing God had to get across to Joshua was that Moses was dead. Joshua certainly knew this, but he probably hadn't fully absorbed its meaning for him. Not to belittle Moses, but he represented the "old" or "former thing" God had done. Joshua used to serve Moses. But now, the time had come for him to lead, a new season in which Joshua had to step up, accept the changing landscape, and do things differently.

His responsibilities and the expectations placed on him by others were changing. He was going to a new level, and that required letting go of the way God had done things with Moses and embracing what God was going to do with him. A repositioning was taking place.

The second thing God had to impress on Joshua was the fact that the Promised Land wasn't going to fall into his lap. He'd not only have to step up but also step in. God was giving the Israelites the land, but they'd have to do their part also. This involved obedient action, because God had clearly said, "Wherever you set foot, you will be on land I have given you."

It's one thing to have a vision for a better future—seeing the promises of God from a distance fills the heart with hope. But what is going to be your response when the promises of God are staring you in the face and it's time to act? There's a sense of comfort in the waiting. However, for the children of Israel, it wasn't just a matter of going into the land and settling. They were going to have to fight for every foot of ground—even though all of it was their inheritance.

This principle also applies to our "promised lands." *The promises of God are there waiting for us, but it's up to us to go in and possess them.* Step up to possess your promise by not only fighting the battles that are ahead, but also the ones that are within: the fears, doubts, and insecurities that, if left unchecked, will seek to hold you back.

God can suddenly shift you from *waiting* on a promise to *walking* in it. But when this happens, you need to be ready to reposition yourself. This makes staying in step with God so invaluable . . . and it requires obedience.

### Don't Drag Your Feet

Lot and the city of Sodom's destruction perfectly illustrate the importance of swift action. Here's a snippet from the story:

> At break of day, the angels pushed Lot to get going, "Hurry. Get your wife and two daughters out of here before it's too late and you're caught in the punishment of the city." Lot was dragging his feet. The men grabbed Lot's arm, and the arms of his wife and daughters—God was so merciful to them!—and dragged them to safety outside the city. When they had them outside, Lot was told, "Now run for your life! Don't look back! Don't stop anywhere on the plain—run for the hills or you'll be swept away." But Lot protested, "No, masters, you can't mean it! I know that you've taken a liking to me and have done me an immense favor in saving my life, but I can't run for the mountains—who knows what terrible thing might happen to me in the mountains and leave me for dead. Look over there—that town is close enough to get to. It's a small town, hardly anything to it. Let me escape there and save my life—it's a mere wide place in the road." "All right, Lot. If you insist. I'll let you have your way. And I won't stamp out the town you've spotted. But hurry up. Run for it! I can't do anything until you get there." That's why the town was called Zoar, that is, Smalltown. (Genesis 19:15–22 MSG)

As we level up, this passage becomes full of more important lessons. Just like we saw with Joshua, stepping up will also require stepping in. And when that time comes, step swiftly, because there's much that remains undone which God yearns to achieve through His people that can only happen when we're willing to act. Does God have free rein to accomplish all He desires through you? With this in mind, let's see what God requires in order for us to do our part.

## Delayed Obedience Is Disobedience

> At break of day, the angels pushed Lot to get going, "Hurry. Get your wife and two daughters out of here before it's too late and you're caught in the punishment of the city." (Genesis 19:15 MSG)

When God instructs us to move, immediate action is required. His directives should never be taken lightly or carelessly—He has zero tolerance for delayed obedience. That doesn't mean God is in a hurry! He will always give you ample time to follow through on His instructions. However, when you procrastinate, He'll warn you to get moving:

> Lot was dragging his feet. The men grabbed Lot's arm, and the arms of his wife and daughters—GOD was so merciful to them!—and dragged them to safety outside the city. (Genesis 19:16 MSG)

Here we find an example of God's mercy. Even when we hesitate, in His grace, God will push us along. Just as an eagle stirs up its nest so that its eaglets learn to fly, so the Lord stirs you up when it's time to level up (see Deuteronomy 32:11–12).

If you're procrastinating, the Lord may uniquely stir your circumstances and disrupt your comfort zone in order to get you moving. However, His intervention may not always be external. Maybe He'll nudge you within your spirit. A sense of restlessness usually follows this type of "nudging" and is only relieved once you carry out God's prompting.

## Identify Your Hesitation

Lot's hesitation was the fear of the unknown:

> "I can't run for the mountains—who knows what terrible thing might happen to me in the mountains and leave me for dead. Look over there—that town is close enough to get to. It's a small town, hardly anything to it. Let me escape there and save my life—it's a mere wide place in the road." "All right, Lot. If you insist. I'll let you have your way." (Genesis 19:18–22 MSG)

Isn't it interesting that God was leading Lot up to the mountains (symbolic for His higher ways and plans), but Lot requested to be sent to "a small town," symbolic of the lower call? Many often settle for less than God's best because they fear the unknown. How sad that we will limit what God wants to do in our life because of fear. In these moments, if we remain stubborn, God will often let us have our way.

*That's why you want to deal with your hesitations because they can kill your dreams.* Refuse to allow anything, or anyone, to stop you from moving into your destiny.

## God Is Waiting on You

> "Hurry up. Run for it! I can't do anything until you get there." (Genesis 19:21–22 MSG)

Many times, we claim we're waiting on God when, really, He's waiting on us. Certain outcomes were contingent upon Lot's obedience.

Likewise, obedience allows God to work in our life. Your action invokes His action.

God's not holding out on you—He's waiting on you! So, don't let not starting stop you!

### Find Your Feet

How many times have you heard this: "It's not how you start, but how you finish that counts." But think about it—you cannot finish what you don't start! Starting counts, too! It's not enough to set our sights on the finish line; we need to push off the starting blocks, too.

I'll never forget the date my son, Leonardo, walked for the first time—Monday, October 3, 2016. Leo's sitter, unable to contain her joy, had told me that Leo started walking during the day. That day I rushed home, all excited, from the office. I could hardly wait to see this milestone for myself.

As Leo's sitter sat with him, from a few feet away I called out to my son, motioning for him to walk. His eyes grew large—and then it happened. He began taking steps. I was stunned! My boy was walking. My mind flashed back to when I was holding him for the first time—it felt like only yesterday! Now, even though he looked like a drunken sailor staggering to find his way back to his ship, I shouted and applauded for him. He walked!

In a similar manner, just as I rejoiced over my son taking his first steps, God also rejoices over your first steps of obedience. The prophet Zechariah's words capture this joy:

> Do not despise these small beginnings, for the LORD rejoices to see the work begin. (Zechariah 4:10 NLT)

The temptation to despise small beginnings is often the result of over-celebrating finishing. Starting doesn't usually provoke the same fanfare as finishing. I'm all about cheering at the finish line. But as we've already established, there cannot be an ending without a beginning. You don't need to start big; you just need to start. And it doesn't matter if you look like a wayward sailor: If you're stepping forward, God rejoices!

What if my son had hesitated to walk because he feared falling? He'd still be crawling. It was his small, shaky steps forward that gave him the strength to eventually find his feet and, later, hit the ground running.

Advancing to new levels can feel like learning to walk. But just as my son found strength taking steps forward, so will you find strength obeying God. You can find your feet as you begin college, enter the workforce, or start a business. No matter what you're beginning, allow yourself to grow into it.

When I began working on writing projects at Messenger International, I was asked to develop an eBook for a course release. It was a small project, but I treated it like a big thing. I was taking small, shaky, baby steps forward that ultimately led to my present role as content director. Those awkward first steps gave me the confidence to take on larger future projects.

Refuse to allow starting to stop you. The smallest step forward can become the biggest step you take. With God, ordinary acts of obedience can lead to extraordinary acts of God.

Here's some encouragement from Dr. Seuss: "You're off to great places! Today is your day! Your mountain is waiting, so . . . get on your way!"

## Put Your Foot Down

> The person who labors, labors for himself, for his hungry mouth drives him on. (Proverbs 16:26)

Hunger is a powerful driving force. It's a mixture of passion, grit, and determination. Hunger is often the catalyst for change that compels us to action. Hunger will disrupt your comfort, shifting you from complacency to desperation. Whether it's the appetite to achieve your goals and dreams or simply survival, one thing is certain: when you're hungry, you cannot remain idle.

As followers of Jesus, our hunger for Him and His kingdom is one of our more precious possessions. This hunger will drive our pursuit of that which God has destined for us, and this hunger won't be satisfied until we taste and see the realities of His purpose and plans for our life. In light of this, Jesus revealed:

> And from the days of John the Baptist until the present time, the kingdom of heaven has endured violent assault, and violent men seize it by force [as a precious prize—a share in the heavenly kingdom is sought with the most ardent zeal and intense exertion]. (Matthew 11:12 AMPC)

The language used in this verse has always intrigued me. Words like "violent assault," "seize it by force," and "precious prize" bounce off the page. These words depict the nature of a God-chaser—one who pursues Him with ardent zeal and intense exertion, viewing the Lord and His plans as a precious prize.

Jacob was such a man. He hungered to fulfill his purpose. He put his foot down and didn't allow anyone or anything to get in his way. Although he's described as a "mild man" in comparison to his brother, Esau, who was "a man of the field," Jacob was not mild when pursuing the things of God. This was apparent even in his mother's womb where Jacob grasped for his brother's heel, competing for the position of firstborn.

Years later, this contention played out, but in a more cunning way. After returning from a day of hunting, Esau was enchanted by the smell of Jacob's stew. Being both tired and starving, Esau begged for a serving. Jacob, who had been waiting for an opportune time, took advantage of his brother by requesting Esau trade his birthright in exchange for a meal. In a moment of weakness, Esau agreed.

Later, after Jacob and Esau's father, Isaac, had grown old and was almost blind, he called on Esau to confer a blessing upon him. But first, Isaac requested that Esau hunt and prepare a final meal for him.

Once Esau had left, Jacob acted quickly, once again taking advantage of the moment. With help from his mother, Rebekah, Jacob deceived his father by disguising himself as Esau and received the blessing that belonged to his brother. After years of desperate pursuit—beginning in the womb—Jacob finally obtained the blessing he had so desired.

When we examine their lives, it's easy to feel sorry for Esau. How would you feel if your brother pulled a "Jacob" on you? But God saw things differently. Hear what God said about them both: "Jacob I have chosen, but Esau I have rejected" (Romans 9:13 TPT).

Why did God make His choice? I believe God chose Jacob, not because of his character—which included manipulation, cheating, and stealing—but because of the value Jacob placed on the blessing of God. He wanted it badly, and he did whatever it took to obtain it. The manner in which Jacob aggressively sought after God's blessing pleased God. Esau's apathy displeased Him.

Many years later, we see Jacob's hunger expressed once again. He wanted more, and this time he was willing to face off with God for it. In what was the defining moment of his life, Jacob wrestled throughout the night with the Lord at Bethel.

> And He said, "Let Me go, for the day breaks." But he (Jacob) said, "I will not let You go unless You bless me!" So He said to him, "What is your name?" He said, "Jacob." And He said, "Your name shall no longer be called Jacob, but Israel; for you have struggled with God and with men and have prevailed." (Genesis 32:26–28, parentheses added)

The imagery that comes to mind when I read this passage is that of a vigilante holding a villain against a wall demanding to know the whereabouts of a bomb's detonator. It's a violent, urgent, no-holds-barred approach. Jacob would not let go until he got what he wanted.

That's the type of hunger God is looking for. A hunger that's willing to put it all on the line. That's the life Jacob exemplified. And because he lived that way, not only was he blessed, but his name—Israel—was the name God chose for His people, those who seize God's kingdom as a special prize.

## Think on Your Feet

As you journey upward through life, having a plan of action is necessary. Plans provide focus and clarity as you navigate your way forward.

> A man's mind plans his way [as he journeys through life], But the LORD directs his steps and establishes them. (Proverbs 16:9 AMP)

Everywhere we go in life, whether it's a vacation or a routine stop by the grocery store, we usually have a planned route to get to our destination. Where these plans go awry is when we make wrong turns or come across roadblocks and detours. When this happens, we must reroute.

Possessing a vision for God's purpose for your life should be accompanied with a plan for how to accomplish it. A vision is for the completed work, while a plan is for completing the work. Rarely does the vision change; on the other hand, rarely do plans ever stay the same. Plans must be frequently reviewed and revised, because of changes caused by unforeseen circumstances and obstacles.

So, when things don't go as planned, don't give up on the vision.

When I moved to America, I tried fulfilling God's vision for my life without revising my plans. This led to many struggles. My internal GPS was crying for a reroute, as I kept driving around in circles! How foolish!

Once I found my feet in new surroundings, I had to develop the skill of thinking on my feet. This meant that I had to respond to changing events decisively, effectively, and without prior thought or planning. I had to grow on the go.

> Commit your works to the LORD [submit and trust them to Him], and your plans will succeed [if you respond to His will and guidance]. (Proverbs 16:3 AMP)

As I've continued to commit my plans to the Lord and respond to His will and guidance, He has faithfully ensured that I step into His plans and purposes for my life. We see an example of this in the apostle Paul's life and missionary journeys:

> They went to Phrygia, and then on through the region of Galatia. Their plan was to turn west into Asia province, but the Holy Spirit blocked that route. So they went to Mysia and tried to go north to Bithynia, but the Spirit of Jesus wouldn't let them go there either. Proceeding on through Mysia, they went down to the seaport Troas. That night Paul had a dream: A Macedonian stood on the far shore and called across the sea, "Come over to Macedonia and help us!" The dream gave Paul his map. We went to work at once getting things ready to cross over to Macedonia. All the pieces had come together. We knew now for sure that God had called us to preach the good news to the Europeans. (Acts 16:6–10 MSG)

Despite his uncertainty of God's will, did you notice that Paul chose to move? He was a man with a plan—a doer and a goer. He was taking steps forward, refusing uncertainty's attempts to stall him. However, he was also sensitive and flexible to the Holy Spirit's leading. He wasn't enslaved to his plan, and therefore he was able to be redirected and repositioned.

Think about it! How much easier is it for the Holy Spirit to steer a moving vessel than one that is stationary? As Paul's heart was set on obeying God's call on his life, the Lord never failed to light his path. However, this clarity wasn't given until Paul took action. God only began speaking and putting the pieces into place, once Paul was on the move.

Each step of obedience you take is like a puzzle piece. As the pieces come together, the big picture is made clearer. In the words of Steve Jobs, "You can't connect the dots looking forward, you can only connect them looking backwards. So you have to trust that the dots will somehow connect in your future."[7]

## On Tiptoe

God's Spirit beckons. There are things to do and places to go! (Romans 8:14 MSG)

There are things God wants us to do and places He wants us to go. This gets me excited about the future, knowing that as we pursue God's will, we'll embark on a thrilling upward adventure with Him. But this adventure requires our active cooperation, following God step by step . . . and sometimes in leaps and bounds. Only then can we level up!

So, let's be on tiptoe, expectant for all that God wants to accomplish through us. For some encouragement along the way, here's a quote by C.S. Lewis: "Isn't it funny how day by day nothing changes, but when you look back everything is different?"[8]

## CHEAT CODE

### Remember
- Leveling up involves more than a change in *position*; it involves a change in *disposition*.
- Change usually requires a new mindset, new habits, new relationships, or learning new things.
- "When God instructs us to move, immediate action is required."
- Restlessness may mean God is nudging you.
- Hesitation can kill dreams.
- It's easier for the Holy Spirit to steer a moving vessel.
- You don't need to start big; just start!

### Reflect
1. Are there areas of disobedience in your life that are hampering your spiritual growth? How might this change?
2. Progress up in our life with God requires hunger, passion, commitment, tenacity, courage. With which of these qualities do you need the Holy Spirit's assistance?

# 7

# LEVERAGE YOUR LEVEL

*Preparation Time Is Never Wasted Time*

Several years after becoming a Christian, I had a riveting dream that has stuck with me ever since.

It was 2005, and I was experiencing an intense time of challenges the Lord was using to refine my character. I had also gone through a relationship breakup and had spiraled into deep discouragement. During that time, I questioned my purpose in life and the direction I was heading, and I almost gave up pursuing my calling in ministry. If it had not been for the warning I'd received, I probably would have quit.

In the dream, I stood alone in the main carriage of a train as it moved steadily along the tracks. After a few minutes, I began to make my way up to the upper deck of the carriage. Every time I placed my foot upon a step, it would glow green. But as I was about to enter the upper carriage, suddenly, I began to fall backward without my feet touching the floor. As this occurred, I looked over my shoulder and saw the lower carriage exterior doors slide open. I was about to fly out when I woke up.

As I awoke, before I could take my first breath, the Holy Spirit gave me the meaning of the dream. It was a warning not to stop pursuing my calling. I was "on track," and He wanted me to stay the course. The train in this dream represented my calling, which I was in. Being a train, it represented that my calling was connected to others both ahead of me and behind me.

As long as I remained in my carriage, I was moving in the right direction and making progress—which was symbolized by the progression up the steps and the green lights, which were symbolic of prospering.

The other interesting fact about this dream was that I was walking up steps, which symbolized that I was going to a new level. But this new level would require obedience, as the Lord directed my steps forward. However, I was at a critical juncture in my life, and the dream came with a warning: if I didn't stay the path, the consequences would be dangerous, which was displayed to me as I was about to leave the carriage and lose the progress I'd made.

The Lord confirmed the dream with Scripture and a book that came across my way. The verse was Leviticus 10:7, which reads, "But you must not leave the entrance of the Tabernacle or you will die, for you have been anointed with the LORD's anointing oil." This statement was spoken by Moses to Aaron's sons, Eleazar and Ithamar, who were newly anointed for priestly service within the Tabernacle, replacing Nadab and Abihu. This was a reminder for me that I was called to serve God within the church and was being warned not to take this calling lightly.

The last confirmation came from a book's title that reiterated the meaning of the dream—*Don't Get Off the Train: En Route to Your Divine Destination*. The Lord's message to me could not have been clearer. The truths and experiences I share in this chapter are a result of the lessons God taught me from this dream, and the importance of staying the course as we progress to new levels of spiritual maturity.

## Trust the Process

Whenever God calls a person, regardless of vocation or the sector of society being called to, He will always take that person through a process, a series of actions and steps in order to achieve a particular end. The process is a transitional period with three distinct stages: a start, a middle, and an end. I identify these stages as *promise, process,* and *promotion.* These stages are cyclical and apply to each level we journey through toward the fulfillment of God's promises for our life. The promise of promotion always goes through a process.

To further explain the process, let's use a car wash as an example. Passing through an automated car wash can be an unnerving experience (at least for me, it is). As you approach the entrance, you must select the type of wash you want and pay for it. (*There is always a cost to God's process, but the promised fulfillment makes it worth it.*) Most car washes offer a variety of options ranging from basic to detailed. Each option promises that your vehicle will be thoroughly cleaned, but the greater the price paid, the more detailing the car will receive—like a coat of wax.

Once you've decided on the wash you want, there's an alignment with the tracking system that's required as you enter the car washing process. This is where you put the car into neutral and you let go of the steering wheel. Once you're in, there's no backing out. (*This is like aligning and surrendering your heart to the work God wants to do in you.*)

As the car wash begins, your vehicle is moved forward by the track system. As the vehicle's driver, you're not required to do anything except yield to the car wash process. While you sit patiently, your vehicle goes through a variety of experiences: it begins to shake as it is bombarded with powerful, spraying water jets, soap is squirted and begins to foam, huge brushes start circulating around your vehicle, sirens and strange noises are buzzing—and all the while, you're like, *What have I got myself into?* (*The process God takes us through can often feel like the experiences we have while in a car wash. But the intended outcome is always for our benefit, so that we emerge as a better version of ourselves.*)

Once the wash is completed, there is absolute silence—the end of the process. Relieved that it's finally over, you are then signaled to make your exit. Mission accomplished—your car is clean! I find that the more times I've experienced the car wash, the less unsettled I am because I've learned to trust the process. *(Likewise, the more we journey with God, the more we learn to trust His ways of dealing with us.)* In relation to God's intentions, the apostle James wrote:

> My brethren, take the prophets, who spoke in the name of the Lord, as an example of suffering and patience. Indeed we count them blessed who endure. You have heard of the perseverance of Job and seen the end *intended by* the Lord—that the Lord is very compassionate and merciful. (James 5:10-11)

God's process will always lead us to the desired destination and outcome, and as this journey unfolds, take heart—you'll see the end intended by the Lord. Paul confidently wrote:

> I'm fully convinced that the One who began this glorious work in you will faithfully continue the process of maturing you and will put His finishing touches to it until the unveiling of our Lord Jesus Christ! (Philippians 1:6 TPT)

Our responsibility is to be as convinced as Paul and to trust the process God is taking us through, confident that He'll complete what He started. We must not rush or abort the process; rather, allow the Lord to accomplish His purpose through it. James also encouraged:

> "So don't try to get out of anything prematurely. Let it do its work, so you become mature and well-developed, not deficient in any way" (James 1:4 MSG).

Imagine if you tried to abort the car wash halfway down the track? Not only would the wash be incomplete, but you would risk damaging your car and possibly being injured. Similarly, when we try to abort or rush the process God has for us, progress is halted and growth is stunted. We frustrate ourselves and prolong our promotion.

## The Value of Experience

> We are assured and know that [God being a partner in their labor] all things work together and are [fitting into a plan] for good to and for those who love God and are called according to [His] design and purpose. (Romans 8:28 AMPC)

Each part of the process is God's plan to prepare you to advance into new levels of your calling. However, on each level, it is important to be aware of the lessons God is teaching you—just like each part of the car wash has a specific role in cleaning your vehicle. Without properly completing each stage, you cannot progress to the next.

One of the valuable outcomes of the process is the experience gained through trials and challenges. Navigating these unique experiences helps prepare you for what God has planned. James provides further insight:

> Consider it nothing but joy, my brothers and sisters, whenever you fall into various trials. Be assured that the testing of your faith [through experience] produces endurance [leading to spiritual maturity, and inner peace]. And let endurance have its perfect result and do a thorough work, so that you may be perfect and completely developed [in your faith], lacking in nothing. (James 1:2–4 AMP)

Certain growth can only occur through *experience*, which is why James encourages us to change our perspective toward the tests and challenges we encounter. They have a purpose. These challenges test what we know and how we're applying what we've learned. The result: We'll grow and develop into our potential.

Even Jesus had to gain experience as a man so that He could effectively fulfill His calling and represent us as High Priest. The writer of Hebrews explains this:

> Although He was a Son, He learned [active, special] obedience through what He suffered and, [His completed experience] making Him perfectly [equipped], He became the Author *and* Source of eternal salvation to all those who give heed and obey Him. (Hebrews 5: 8–9 AMPC)

It wasn't sufficient for Jesus only to know about the human condition—He also had to experience it. Notice that after His "completed experience," He was perfectly equipped for His promotion and role as High Priest. That's why you shouldn't devalue what you're presently going through. You're acquiring experience that will be needed as you progress to new levels of destiny.

There's great value to gaining experience. Look at what Solomon shared:

> Happy [blessed, considered fortunate, to be admired] is the man who finds [skillful and godly] wisdom, and the man who gains understanding and insight [learning from God's word and life's experiences] . . . (Proverbs 3:13 AMP)

There's a big difference between education and experience. And we need both. Employers don't just look for what you know; they look for what you can do. Experience offers the opportunity to demonstrate what you can produce, where you can show how you apply what you know. That's why internships and apprenticeships are such a great way to make progress in your calling—they offer valuable experience that educational institutes cannot provide.

God's process is similar to an apprenticeship or internship, as He trains and equips you for your calling. The psalmist expressed:

I will praise and give thanks to You with uprightness of heart when I learn [by sanctified experiences] Your righteous judgments [Your decisions against and punishments for particular lines of thought and conduct]. (Psalm 119:7 AMPC)

I love the idea of learning through "sanctified experiences." It carries the notion that certain experiences are tailor-made to suit your calling and preparation process. I titled this chapter *Leverage Your Level* because when we have the attitude of maximizing and taking advantage of our current level, we'll prepare ourselves for new levels.

To illustrate this point, imagine a virtual video game. With any good video game, it is necessary to complete multiple levels before ultimately completing the game. Each level consists of unique battles to engage and specific items to collect. The goal is not to get through a level quickly but to acquire the hidden items unique to that level, all the while successfully combating the opposition that seeks to hinder your progress. What is obtained on one level is most often needed on the next.

Drawing from this analogy, it is crucial that we fully engage in the present moment. It's easy to become consumed with a desired destination and lose sight of what God is presently doing to help get you there. How we steward our present season greatly affects the way we step into the future.

Growth, not speed, is our aim.

## Private Victories

Gaining experience involves private victories. And those private victories will ultimately become publicly evident, as everything we go through shapes who we are.

David's private victories, and how they played a pivotal role for him publicly, are found in 1 Samuel 17 where King Saul and his army are paralyzed by fear, because the Philistine giant, Goliath, is taunting them day and night.

David's father, Jesse, asks him to visit his brothers on the frontlines of battle. When David arrives, he's appalled by the lack of action and volunteers to fight Goliath:

> "Master," said David, "don't give up hope. I'm ready to go and fight this Philistine." Saul answered David, "You can't go and fight this Philistine. You're too young and inexperienced—and he's been at this fighting business since before you were born."
> (1 Samuel 17:32–33 MSG)

Saul had no idea who David was nor was he aware of the abilities he possessed. Saul viewed David as a young and inexperienced boy. But David was battle-ready, for he had prepared for this moment in private, having gained experience in battle that no one knew about. He responded:

> "I've been a shepherd, tending sheep for my father. Whenever a lion or bear came and took a lamb from the flock, I'd go after it, knock it down, and rescue the lamb. If it turned on me, I'd grab it by the throat, wring its neck, and kill it. Lion or bear, it made no difference—I killed it. And I'll do the same to this Philistine pig who is taunting the troops of God-Alive. GOD, who delivered me from the teeth of the lion and the claws of the bear, will deliver me from this Philistine." Saul said, "Go. And GOD help you!"
> (1 Samuel 17:34–37 MSG)

David's confidence was not a result of arrogance or youthful zeal, but rather based on the experience he'd gained with God in private. David had gained experience on one level, and through this pending victory, he'd gain access to another.

As the story unfolded, David killed Goliath, winning a huge victory for Israel. From this public exposure, David gained fame and was promoted into Saul's army. The very day he defeated Goliath, David was elevated from the pastures to the palace. It literally took getting a head to get ahead!

## Progress Through the Process

In regard to fulfilling your destiny, I cannot emphasize this enough: *Between a promise and its fulfillment, there is always a process.*

We see an example of this process in the life of Elisha, so let's glean insight from his journey found in 2 Kings 2:1–13. The story picks up in Gilgal, from where Elisha received his calling, and culminates at the Jordan River, where he received his commissioning.

> And it came to pass, when the LORD was about to take up Elijah into heaven by a whirlwind, that Elijah went with Elisha from Gilgal. Then Elijah said to Elisha, "Stay here, please, for the LORD has sent me on to Bethel." But Elisha said, "As the LORD lives, and *as* your soul lives, I will not leave you!" So they went down to Bethel.
>
> Now the sons of the prophets who *were* at Bethel came out to Elisha, and said to him, "Do you know that the LORD will take away your master from over you today?" And he said, "Yes, I know; keep silent!"
>
> Then Elijah said to him, "Elisha, stay here, please, for the LORD has sent me on to Jericho." But he said, "As the LORD lives, and *as* your soul lives, I will not leave you!" So they came to Jericho.
>
> Now the sons of the prophets who *were* at Jericho came to Elisha and said to him, "Do you know that the LORD will take away your master from over you today?" So he answered, "Yes, I know; keep silent!"
>
> Then Elijah said to him, "Stay here, please, for the LORD has sent me on to the Jordan." But he said, "As the LORD lives, and *as* your soul lives, I will not leave you!" So the two of them went on.

And fifty men of the sons of the prophets went and stood facing *them* at a distance, while the two of them stood by the Jordan. Now Elijah took his mantle, rolled *it* up, and struck the water; and it was divided this way and that, so that the two of them crossed over on dry ground.

And so it was, when they had crossed over, that Elijah said to Elisha, "Ask! What may I do for you, before I am taken away from you?" Elisha said, "Please let a double portion of your spirit be upon me."

So he said, "You have asked a hard thing. *Nevertheless,* if you see me *when I am* taken from you, it shall be so for you; but if not, it shall not be *so.*"

Then it happened, as they continued on and talked, that suddenly a chariot of fire *appeared* with horses of fire, and separated the two of them; and Elijah went up by a whirlwind into heaven.

And Elisha saw *it,* and he cried out, "My father, my father, the chariot of Israel and its horsemen!" So he saw him no more. And he took hold of his own clothes and tore them into two pieces. He also took up the mantle of Elijah that had fallen from him, and went back and stood by the bank of the Jordan.

After reading this account, we see four specific places mentioned: Gilgal, Bethel, Jericho, and the Jordan. I believe that each of these four places is symbolic and has prophetic application to aid our understanding of the process between calling and commissioning. The first is Gilgal, which I believe symbolizes a place of consecration and commitment. The name "Gilgal" literally means "separation." When we recall the history of the children of Israel, led by Joshua, Gilgal was the place where the second generation coming out of Egypt renewed the Abrahamic covenant through circumcision. Thus, they recommitted themselves to the God of Israel before entering the Promised Land.

Gilgal is also the place where Elisha received his calling to become Elijah's successor. In 1 Kings 19:19–21, we find Elisha committing himself to follow Elijah, which was evident when he burned his plowing equipment and used it as an altar to sacrifice his oxen to the Lord. This action signified that he was letting go of his past and separating himself unto the Lord's service.

The second location Elisha found himself in was Bethel, which I believe is symbolic for encountering God for yourself. Bethel means "house of God." It's the place where Jacob encountered God in a dream (Genesis 28:10–22) and saw a ladder extended from earth to heaven with angels ascending and descending. Within the dream, God spoke with Jacob and confirmed His covenant with him. When he awoke, Jacob expressed:

> "Surely the LORD is in this place, and I did not know it." And he was afraid and said, "How awesome is this place! This is none other than the house of God, and this is the gate of heaven!" (Genesis 28:16–17)

The third place Elisha journeyed to was Jericho, which I believe symbolizes warfare and growth. I immediately think of Israel conquering the nation of Jericho and how its walls came tumbling down (see Joshua 6). During this time, Israel learned how to fight the Lord's battles by yielding to His unconventional methods of combat.

For six days, their worship team led the march of the Israelites around the city of Jericho. Then, on the seventh day, after they marched around seven times, the walls came down and they conquered the city. This is how we learn to do things God's way, which often contradicts traditional methods. Here we learn to trust God and grow in our faith.

The last place in the process was the Jordan River, which is symbolic for promotion and transition. The Jordan is where Elisha received a double portion of Elijah's anointing and was commissioned as Israel's prophet in Elijah's place. And, of course, the Jordan is also where Jesus was baptized, filled with the Holy Spirit, and began His earthly ministry.

Each of these four places—Gilgal (commitment; consecration),

Bethel (encounter), Jericho (warfare; growth), and the Jordan (promotion; transition)—represent four unique purposes for the process God takes us through. You'll find that these four purposes complement and build upon each other.

With every level, we'll renew our commitment to the Lord's service. This will also require a fresh encounter with God, because it's important not to rely on past experiences but to continually engage God in fresh ways.

Every new level requires new growth. I've heard it said, "new level, new devil."

In order to make progress through the process, we must adopt the no-quit attitude exemplified by Elisha. Whenever Elijah was ready to move on, Elisha's resolve was tested. But Elisha refused to stay behind, and always responded with, "As the Lord lives, and as your soul lives, I will not leave you!"

These words carry the fiery determination needed to level up and make the progress God desires for us. If we lack this resolve, we'll find ourselves becoming complacent and stuck, stifling our growth.

According to scholars, Elisha's journey serving alongside Elijah took approximately twelve years. Within that time, I'm sure Elisha had many opportunities to quit. God looks to see if we'll follow Him all the way and obey to the completion of our maturity.

This same passion was evident in the apostle Paul, who never settled for what he had accomplished, but kept pressing on to his higher calling:

> Not that I have already attained, or am already perfected; but I press on, that I may lay hold of that for which Christ Jesus has also laid hold of me. Brethren, I do not count myself to have apprehended; but one thing I do, forgetting those things which are behind and reaching forward to those things which are ahead, I press toward the goal for the prize of the upward call of God in Christ Jesus. (Philippians 3:12–14)

If we are going to progress successfully, we, too, must keep pressing forward. To "press" implies that we'll encounter resistance. Pursuing God's higher calling is never easy, but it's totally worth it. Keep giving yourself to the process so that you can keep progressing!

## The Value of Buying

The Bible reveals two ways we can receive from God. Some things are *given* to us, and some things are *bought*. I'm so thankful for the things that are freely given to us—salvation, forgiveness, mercy, grace, God's Spirit—the list of these gifts is long. God is a giver, and He loves to pour out His blessings lavishly upon us: "No good *thing* will He withhold from those who walk uprightly" (Psalm 84:11).

There are certain things, however, that are bought with a price. Jesus exhorted the church in Laodicea, "I counsel you to *buy from Me* gold refined in the fire, that you may be rich" (Revelation 3:18). Jesus didn't say to believe and receive gold refined in the fire; He said to buy that gold. It has a price.

Naturally, we tend to value and appreciate things we've bought more than things we've been given. This really hit home for me when I made the transition from a renter to a homeowner. As a renter, I took care of the places where I lived, but I never fully invested myself and my resources into those homes, because I didn't buy and own them. If something broke or was damaged, I'd call maintenance and they'd come and fix it at no cost to me.

But that changed once I bought a home. I now spent money on things I didn't have to as renter, and if something broke or was damaged, guess who paid for it now? Everything became so much more valuable because it had a price tag on it. And since I was invested, there's also more emotion attached to my home.

Here's another example. Imagine two teenage boys who've just gotten their driver's licenses. One is given a car by his parents, while the other has to work and save up to purchase his car. Who do you think will value and appreciate his car more? The one who had to pay a price for it! It's the same way with the things of God.

When God requires us to buy things, how do we make payment? The currency is *the giving of ourselves*.

About this method of payment, Paul wrote that we are no longer our own: "You were God's expensive purchase, paid for with tears of blood" (1 Corinthians 6:20 TPT). The price tag for us was Jesus. He bought us by giving Himself for us. Likewise, we also buy things by giving ourselves. The price you're willing to pay for something reveals the value you place on it. If we value all that God has for us through the process, we'll freely lay our lives down to obtain it.

Returning to the Lord's words to the Laodiceans, let's take a look at this gold we are to purchase. First, it's a purified faith. Peter wrote:

> These trials will show that your faith is genuine. It is being tested as fire tests and purifies gold—though your faith is far more precious than mere gold. So when your faith remains strong through many trials, it will bring you much praise and glory and honor on the day when Jesus Christ is revealed to the whole world. (1 Peter 1:7 NLT)

The second quality of this gold is refined character. Job said, "But He knows the way that I take [and He pays attention to it]. *When* He has tried me, I will come forth as [refined] gold [pure and luminous]" (Job 23:10 AMP).

Just like gold is refined by fire, our faith and character are refined by the fire of tests and trials, through the growth process. Our tests and trials are an opportunity to buy spiritual gold. But once again, these things can only happen as we give ourselves to God's process. That's how we buy a purified faith and Christlike character, and we'll safeguard them as costly valuables—remembering all we went through to obtain what money cannot buy.

Most of us go to great lengths to protect our valuables. The same activity should apply to our spiritual possessions obtained through God's process.

## Pay the Price

Throughout life, we constantly make tradeoffs, gaining things at the cost of other things. Paul said he was letting go of the past (victories included) and reaching forward to what lies ahead (see Philippians 3:12–13). When it comes to leveling up, we also need to give up in order to go up.

We just examined how Elisha paid the price to progress to new levels in his calling. Esau was an example of someone who didn't . . . and how it cost him dearly:

> Watch out for the Esau syndrome: trading away God's lifelong gift in order to satisfy a short-term appetite. You well know how Esau later regretted that impulsive act and wanted God's blessing—but by then it was too late, tears or no tears. (Hebrews 12:16 MSG)

Many, like Esau, have failed to enter into all God had destined for them because they sold themselves short, choosing the path of least resistance. You, too, will have to resist temptations that will cause you to compromise your calling, each temptation having one objective: to derail you from the process to promotion.

I shared at the beginning of this chapter how, early in my walk with God, I was tempted to give up on pursuing the Lord's plan for my life. If it had not been for God's mercy given to me through that dream, I would've traded away future blessings for temporary satisfaction. I cringe at how close I came to doing that!

Jesus offered the solution to avoid this trap:

"Anyone who intends to come with me has to let me lead. You're not in the driver's seat; *I* am. Don't run from suffering; embrace it. Follow me and I'll show you how. Self-help is no help at all. Self-sacrifice is the way, my way, to finding yourself, your true self. What kind of deal is it to get everything you want but lose yourself? What could you ever trade your soul for? (Matthew 16:24–26 MSG)

Letting Jesus lead means embracing the hard things, not running from them. Self-sacrifice is the way to entering into all He has destined for you.

Advancing to new levels will cost you! That's because the plan of God is an installment plan. If you want to move forward with God's plan for your life, it will require payments and sacrifices. That's why we must always count the cost.

One thing is certain: With God, you'll always gain more than what you give up.

## Stay the Course

Be like those who stay the course with committed faith and then get everything promised to them . . . So don't throw it all away now. You were sure of yourselves then. It's *still* a sure thing! But you need to stick it out, staying with God's plan so you'll be there for the promised completion. (Hebrews 6:12; 10:36 MSG)

God's plans for you are a sure thing . . . as long as you stick around long enough for the promised completion. Mistaking the rewards of the world's success for true success is one reason people abort the process. They fail to realize how far they've come and how close they are to the goal.

In his book, *Visioneering*, Andy Stanley wrote:

Success is remaining faithful to the process God has laid out for you. Certainly there are significant and enjoyable mile markers along the way. But success is not the mile marker. Success is not the raise, promotion, recognition . . . Success is staying faithful to the process that contributed to those things becoming a reality.[9]

From the verses in Hebrews 6 and 10, two phrases equally emphasize receiving what God has promised: "Stay the course" and "Staying with God's plan." The key word is *stay*. God's process to fulfill His promise often takes longer than we expect. That's because God is not in a rush and operates on His own timetable, not ours.

Don't miss what God has for you because you're unwilling to stay the course. Keep making progress. Keep paying the price. It will all be worth it in the end.

## CHEAT CODE

### Remember
- "Between a promise and its fulfillment, there is always a process."
- The timing and time involved in a process is up to God.
- Each level of the process includes lessons to learn.
- A "sanctified experience" is one that is tailor-made to assist you in your calling.
- There's a cost to advancing to a new level with God. *Stay the course.*

### Reflect
1. How easy or difficult is it for you to trust God's process with your life? List reasons for your answer.
2. How is God using your current circumstances to prepare you for the next "Level Up" with Him?

# 8

# UP YOUR GAME

*It's What You Do in the Dark That Makes You Shine in the Light*

Each of us are uniquely called and gifted by God in order to effectively function in our calling.

If you're called to be an athlete, it's only natural that you're gifted with athletic ability. If you're called to the realm of finance, you'll have a particular way with numbers. Our gifts will always complement our callings.

Another aspect to consider is that our gifts also play a significant role in helping us realize our potential and grow into our calling. In regard to this, Solomon wrote, "A man's gift *makes room* for him, and brings him before great men" (Proverbs 18:16).

Your gift makes room or "space" for you. The "space" I'm talking about is twofold. First, your gift makes room for you to fulfill your potential—bridging the space between *where you are* and *where you could be*. Second, your gift creates a pathway to promotion. In other words, your gift makes room for you to be promoted to new levels of your destiny. And with every promotion, a higher standard of skill is required.

Again, Solomon wrote, "If you are uniquely gifted in your work, you will rise and be promoted. You won't be held back—you'll stand before kings!" (Proverbs 22:29 TPT). So, we clearly see that your gifts are pivotal to fulfilling your calling.

Consider David. In 1 Samuel 16, we find the account of Saul being tormented by an evil spirit, because the Spirit of the Lord had departed from him. Desperate for relief, Saul orders one of his servants to seek a skilled musician who might play and comfort him. With a nod of affirmation, Saul's servant responds:

> "'I know someone. I've seen him myself: the son of Jesse of Bethlehem, an excellent musician. He's also courageous, of age, well-spoken, and good looking. And God is with him'" (1 Samuel 16:18 MSG).

I can imagine this whole scenario: Saul summons his servant to find an excellent musician to rock out for him. You have to remember; they didn't have Spotify or Apple Music back then. His servant—already having someone in mind—replies, "Oh, no problem. I know someone!" Immediately, he thinks of David—the long-haired, bearded heartthrob—with his skinny jeans, deep-V sheepskin tunic, and the recent winner of *Israel's Got Talent*. I can just picture David walking around town, with his hair blowing in the wind, singing, "Livin' on a Prayer" or "God Gave Rock and Roll to You"!

But in all seriousness, David wasn't just a gifted musician; he was a skilled one. And because his gift was developed, room was made for him to advance in his calling. Later, as seen in the Psalms, we see David's songwriting gift emerge. These songs, for the most part, were written and developed in private.

With this in mind, could it be that many are not progressing in their calling because their gifts are underdeveloped? Could the degree to which our gifts are developed determine the extent in which we can be promoted?

One of the gifts in my life is writing. Since moving to America, I have invested many hours practicing and developing this craft. At first, this began in private, but eventually became my full-time role at Messenger International.

When I first started to get serious about writing, I wrote a blog every week. If I'm honest, I knew the blog wasn't for anything else other than the development of my gift. Each week I diligently recorded my thoughts and revelations in a structured way. The more committed I remained to this habit, the better I became. As I continued to practice, my capacity to receive revelation and to write grew. Looking back, I was being faithful with the little I had, and more was periodically being given to me.

After about a year of doing this, the Lord put it on my heart to write a book. I had a core theme and an outline, and the urge to write was stronger than the resistance not to. I moved from writing a blog per week to writing a chapter per week. I completed the initial manuscript in approximately three months. Although nothing came about with this book, I was stirring up my gift to write. My skill as a writer was growing and developing. I had tapped into an area of gifting that was dormant.

About a year later, I began to write another book. Again, I had a core theme and inspiration to do so. This time, however, I self-published the book as an eBook on Amazon. This was a breakthrough moment. Even though the book didn't sell well, I was so proud of myself. For the first time, I had seen a writing project to completion and learned a lot. It was a personal victory.

While my gift to write began to grow and mature, opportunities to do writing projects at Messenger International grew as well. They began small, but as I continued to give my all to these assignments, more was entrusted to me. My gift began to make room for me to step into a full-time position to write and develop content on behalf of John and Lisa Bevere. Now, I've written a third book, and Messenger International has published it.

What I've discovered through all this is that your gift will definitely make room for you to advance to new levels of destiny. When you remain faithful and diligent to developing your gift, you'll find yourself rising and being promoted.

## Excel

One of my great joys is to watch people excel in their giftings. No matter where you look—sports, entertainment, government, business, ministry—you'll find people excelling in their giftings, astounding us by what they do and how well they do it. Perhaps your heart skipped a beat listening to Whitney Houston's rendition of "The Star-Spangled Banner" during Super Bowl XXV, or when America stood still during the 2016 Olympic Games in Rio de Janeiro as swimmer Michael Phelps won five gold medals.

When we observe these individuals, it's easy to compare ourselves with them and assume their success is due to having been born with something extra. And because we haven't witnessed them perfecting their gift in private, it's easy to overlook all the hard work they put in to perform the way they do. The reality is we, too, possess gifts. And we're all given the opportunity to excel in our areas of strength. For this reason, Paul wrote to Timothy, "Do not *neglect* the gift that is in you, which was given to you by prophecy with the laying on of the hands of the eldership" (1 Timothy 4:14).

Paul begins by warning Timothy not to *neglect* his gift. When we neglect our gifts, they remain dormant and our growth is stunted, holding us back from realizing our potential. There are many reasons our gifts can be neglected, but the most common is that we often covet someone else's gift, despising our own. *It's critical we develop the gifts we have, not the gifts we want.*

It always makes me cringe when I see someone pursuing an area of gifting that's clearly not their area of strength. This doesn't mean we can't acquire other skills or abilities—as long as you're not neglecting development of your areas of strength. We can all heed the advice given by Theodore Roosevelt: "Your ability needs responsibility to expose its possibilities."

After Paul warned Timothy to keep his gift dusted off and active, he then coached him on how to develop it:

"Practice *and* cultivate *and* meditate upon these duties; throw yourself wholly into them [as your ministry], so that your progress may be evident to everybody" (1 Timothy 4:15 AMPC).

Timothy's progress would become evident as he fully invested himself into his calling through practice, cultivation (coaching), and meditation (reflection). Let's briefly examine each of these.

## Practice

Our private practice will determine our public performance. Practice involves being professionally engaged in our craft. In other words, we're taking the development of our gifts seriously. It's easy to marvel at someone's performance lasting several minutes and lose sight of the weeks, months, and years of training and hard work that went into consistently performing at such a high level.

According to experts in the science of human behavior and performance, it takes approximately 10,000 hours of practice to become proficient or a master in a particular skill. Professor K. Anders Ericsson of Florida State University challenges traditional beliefs that practice makes perfect, and he takes it a step further by revealing that it's not enough to practice for 10,000 hours, unless those hours of practice are done with focused intention to improve, rather than just going through the motions. He coined this type of practice as *purposeful practice*. He wrote:

> So here we have purposeful practice in a nutshell: Get outside your comfort zone but do it in a focused way, with clear goals, a plan for reaching those goals, and a way to monitor your progress. Oh, and figure out a way to maintain your motivation.[10]

Unless we push beyond our level of comfort and skill, we'll never grow. The danger is that once we reach a level of "good enough," we can easily become complacent. Then it's only a matter of time before we become sloppy in our practice, which will ultimately have a negative effect on our performance.

In 2015, Under Armour launched its global marketing campaign, "Rule Yourself," which centered around the concept of *"It's what you do in the dark that puts you in the light."* The campaign showcased several of Under Armour's athletes training in pursuit of athletic greatness. One of them was American swimmer Michael Phelps, one of America's most celebrated athletes, who was coming back for one last hurrah after he'd retired at the top of his game in 2012.

The commercial captured him diligently preparing for the 2016 Olympic Games, giving us a glimpse into his private preparation that had earned him his Olympic stardom. As I've already noted, Phelps went on to win five more gold medals, capping his career off with twenty-eight Olympic medals. What he did in the dark definitely was rewarded in the light.

Since its release in 2015, the *Rule Yourself* video featuring Michael Phelps has had over 10 million views (and counting) worldwide. Could the popularity of this ad be due to the fact that it reveals Phelps's humanity? When we're given a glimpse into what goes on behind the camera, it strikes a chord deep within our heart that inspires us to believe that we, too, can achieve high performance . . . if we put in the work.

The apostle Paul, who was steeped in a culture that celebrated human performance and achievement, wrote:

> A true athlete will be disciplined in every respect, practicing constant self-control in order to win a laurel wreath that quickly withers. But we run our race to win a victor's crown that will last forever. For that reason, I don't run just for exercise or box like one throwing aimless punches, but I train like a champion athlete. I subdue my body and get it under my control, so that after preaching the good news to others I myself won't be disqualified. (1 Corinthians 9:25–27 TPT)

Paul contrasts the Christian life to that of an athlete, pointing out that, just as an athlete will be disciplined and must practice constant self-control, so must we. Just as Paul did, we must train like a champion athlete in regard to our calling and gifts. Athletes train to win earthly crowns, but we work for eternal crowns. That's the prize of the upward call of God that Paul was talking about (see Philippians 3:14).

In regard to the importance of practice, leadership expert John Maxwell wrote:

> "It has been my observation that people can increase their ability by 2 points on a scale of 1–10. For example, if your natural talent in an area is a 4, with hard work you may rise to a 6. In other words, you go from being a little below average to a little above average. But let's say you find a place where you are a 7; you have the potential to become a 9, maybe even a 10, if it's your greatest area of strength and you work exceptionally hard."[11]

Developing your area of strength is liberating, not limiting. Once again, this does not mean we don't develop our areas of weakness or acquire new skills. It does mean we're focused and invested in the areas that will yield the greatest return in our potential. Here's the bottom line: Growth is not automatic; it requires intentionality.

Unless we're consistently practicing so that we can develop our gifts, we'll never realize our full potential. That's why we must remain committed to personal growth. Most people want to do great things with their life, but not everyone is willing to put in the necessary work to become great. Practice is paying the price that produces great reward.

## Coaching

Practice is practical, while cultivating is more educational. When you consider the word *cultivate*, think of coaching. Coaching is critical to your personal growth and development as it provides constructive criticism and guidance that cannot be acquired on your own. Anyone who has excelled in their gifting has had coaching and guidance from others. The wonderful element of having a coach is that—much more so than you—they see your potential and are committed to draw it out of you. A great example of coaching is evident in NBC's popular TV show *The Voice*. After advancing from the blind auditions, contestants are given the opportunity to choose a celebrity coach to team with throughout the show. The most enjoyable aspect of the program—despite the jaw-dropping performances—is watching how the growth of the contestants is expedited by gleaning insight from their coaches who are further along in their own gifting. Coaching can come through mentor-mentee relationships, apprenticeships, internships, and indirectly from books, courses, and an abundance of other resources.

Another way to receive education in your gifting is to gather with those who share similar giftings—"find your tribe"—where you can collaborate and innovate together.

Citing another example from NBC, *Songland* is a songwriting competition that hosts a celebrity artist in search for their next hit song. Four songwriters are invited into the studio to perform their song in front of the artist and three well-known songwriters. Three are chosen to partner and collaborate with the other songwriters.

Once their songs are tweaked, edited, and produced, contestants are then given another opportunity to perform their song. The celebrity artist then selects the winner, which often results in their song becoming a hit. The most entertaining aspect about this program is witnessing the development of a song through the collaboration of other gifted songwriters. This aspect of the music industry is often overlooked.

### Reflection

At its core, to meditate means to reflect or to contemplate. When it comes to the development of our giftings, certain growth occurs only when we take time to stop and reflect on the lessons we're learning.

When we honestly monitor our growth and allow time to evaluate our progress and performance, we become aware of the specific areas that need attention or improvement. This practice is often seen with athletes reviewing hours of tape analyzing, critiquing, and dissecting different aspects of their performance.

During my role as content manager, I've received consistent feedback and constructive criticism for my writing. Addison, who's the COO at Messenger, has coached me as a writer and taken the time to pour himself into me. As a result of his wisdom, my growth has accelerated.

It's interesting when I look back on projects that I worked on a year or two ago, I think, *How did I think this was any good?* Sometimes it's difficult to review my previous work because of how much I've grown since then. And that's what keeps me encouraged and moving forward. If I'm not better today than I was yesterday, I'm not progressing.

When we monitor our growth and allow time to evaluate our progress and performance, we become aware of the specific areas that need attention or improvement. Leadership expert John Maxwell often reminds his audiences and readers that experience is not the best teacher—evaluated experience is.

As you reflect on your progress, take to heart the feedback you receive from coaches and peers, and think of innovative ways to improve and utilize your gifts. Ask yourself the right questions: What do I need to change? What have been my biggest areas of growth? What are the areas I need to give more attention to? What is required for me to break through to a new level?

Reflection time is never wasted time.

### The Grace Advantage

Before ending this chapter, I'd like to briefly bring up performance-enhancing substances. Throughout history, whether during ancient battles or the Olympic Games, mankind has always sought ways to boost its competitive edge and gain an advantage over foes. This often leads to the use of performance-enhancing substances, such as steroids and human growth hormones. In most organized sports, the use of such substances is banned. Since these rules are frequently ignored and overlooked, more athletes are cheating.

The apostle Paul was aware of a performance-enhancing substance, one that was high-quality, readily accessible, and free—and that came with no side effects! No, he didn't use steroids or human growth hormones! The substance that gave him an edge was the grace of God. Paul revealed:

> But God's amazing grace has made me who I am! And his grace to me was not fruitless. In fact, I worked harder than all the rest, yet not in my own strength but God's, for his empowering grace is poured out upon me. (1 Corinthians 15:10 TPT)

Paul credited his accomplishments and his ability to outperform his peers to the grace of God. True, he worked harder than all the apostles, but he also had an unfair advantage. He admitted, "not in my own strength." What? So where did his strength come from? He said, "not in my own strength but God's."

Paul had a revelation of grace that seemed different from that of the other apostles. We gain more insight into this from his discourse with Jesus. Each time He said:

> "My grace is all you need. My power works best in weakness." So now I am glad to boast about my weaknesses, so that the power of Christ can work through me. (2 Corinthians 12:9 NLT)

In this situation, Paul was pleading with the Lord for help against the thorn in his flesh (which scholars believe was a demonic foe). In response, Jesus revealed that what he needed was not an intervention, but rather a dose of the Lord's grace. Jesus contrasted grace with power: "My *grace* is all you need. My *power* works best in weakness."

What many believers have failed to understand is that God's grace is more than mercy; it's a powerful substance that empowers us to perform beyond our natural ability. With this fresh insight, Paul became a grace junkie! He gloried in his weaknesses because they qualified him for grace. Read these Scriptures with this fresh perspective on grace:

> I can do all things [which He has called me to do] through Him who strengthens *and* empowers me [to fulfill His purpose—I am self-sufficient in Christ's sufficiency; I am ready for anything and equal to anything through Him who infuses me with inner strength and confident peace.] (Philippians 4:13 AMP)
>
> For He Who motivated *and* fitted Peter *and* worked effectively through him for the mission to the circumcised, motivated *and* fitted me *and* worked through me also for [the mission to] the Gentiles. (Galatians 2:8 AMPC)
>
> "I have been made a messenger of this wonderful news by the gift of grace that works through me. Even though I am the least significant of all his holy believers, this grace-gift was imparted when the manifestation of his power came upon me. Grace alone empowers me so that I can boldly preach this wonderful message to non-Jewish people, sharing with them the unfading, inexhaustible riches of Christ, which are beyond comprehension. (Ephesians 3:7–8 TPT)

The common thread among these sample passages is that grace is a performance-enhancer. Through grace, we're empowered to fulfill our specific and unique purpose, and we're equipped with gifts to function effectively in our purpose. So then, how do we begin accessing and functioning in performance-enhancing grace? The answer is simple: by faith.

Faith activates grace: "we have access by faith into this grace in which we stand" (Romans 5:2). But in order to have faith, we must know what God's Word says about grace. When we limit grace to only mercy, we'll only have faith for mercy. But when we understand that grace also "empowers" us, we'll have faith for grace to energize us. Paul also shared:

> God's marvelous grace imparts to each one of us varying gifts and ministries that are uniquely ours. So if God has given you the grace-gift of prophecy, you must activate your gift by using the proportion of faith you have to prophesy. (Romans 12:6 TPT)

There we have it again: faith activates grace. All of these verses I've shared about grace were written by Paul. He wanted everyone to know what was so amazing about grace! Apparently, no other apostle had such a robust revelation of grace. That's the reason he bore more fruit than his peers—he had an advantage!

You, too, can gain an advantage, not to be better than others, but to become better than you presently are. By faith, recognize your need and depend on God's grace to supply what's lacking.

## Hold Nothing Back

> Practice *and* cultivate *and* meditate upon these duties; throw yourself wholly into them [as your ministry], so that your progress may be evident to everybody. (1 Timothy 4:15 AMPC)

Everything we've discussed is contingent upon giving ourselves completely to what God has called and gifted us to do. Your calling demands your full commitment. As we give ourselves wholeheartedly to what God has entrusted to us, our progress will be obvious, and we'll continue to rise to new levels of growth and achievement. Paul described this in his letter to the believers in Galatia:

> Make a careful exploration of who you are and the work you have been given and then sink yourself into that. Don't be impressed with yourself. Don't compare yourself to others. Each of you must

take responsibility for doing the creative best you can with your own life. (Galatians 6:4–5 MSG)

Each of us are responsible for stewarding our gifts and doing our creative best with our own life. We've seen that the degree to which our gifts are developed will determine the levels we can reach in our calling. We have one shot at this life to realize our potential. Let's pursue personal growth and development.

If we're not progressing, we're regressing.

Bottom line: When you discover your gift, you'll move in the right direction. But when you develop your gift, you'll rise in the right direction—advancing to new levels.

## CHEAT CODE

### Remember
- "Your private practice will determine your public performance."
- Athletes train to win *earthly* crowns; we work for *eternal* crowns.
- Coaching and guidance from others help us excel in our gifting.
- Time invested in reflection of our progress and growth is never wasted.
- Grace is more than mercy—it's also a performance-enhancer.

### Reflect
1. What are your God-given gifts?
2. How might the power of grace expand in your life so that your gifts will influence your spheres of influence?

# 9

# A HAND UP

*Mentors Will Help Move You
from Where You Are to
Where You Want to Go*

Known for their uncanny ability to scale Himalayan peaks, Tibetan Sherpas are highly skilled and experienced climbers. For the avid mountain climber, having the assistance and expertise of a Sherpa is invaluable. Every year, hundreds of climbers visit the Himalayan region in an attempt to summit Mount Everest. Sherpas are hired to prepare specific routes, set ropes in place, and carry the necessary climbing gear up the mountain while foreign climbers follow their lead. Without a Sherpa's help, reaching the top of Everest is almost an impossible feat, even for the most seasoned mountaineers.

In a way similar to climbers receiving help from Sherpas, our upward journey with God also requires assistance from those who are more experienced. This help will come from mentors, spiritual fathers and mothers, and coaches who can give us a hand up as we scale different levels of our destiny. Their assistance must be sought out diligently and applied faithfully. Like a skilled Sherpa, they'll help us navigate our way forward by providing wisdom, leadership, and modeling.

## The Transporter

A good mentor is a guide, a pathfinder, a waymaker. They're a transporter—a person who will help move you from where you are to where you want to go. And they also desire for you to go further than they've gone themselves. They show the way forward and provide you with the needed fuel to go the distance.

In different nations and cultures, mentors have a variety of names and titles. These include sensei, rabbi, maestro, advisor, and coach. The most commonly used term for a mentor these days is a coach. In his book, *Aspire*, Kevin Hall explains the origin of the word "coach":

> Originally crafted for aristocracy, coaches carried important people to their desired destinations in luxury and ease. Their compact, sturdy, and elegant design far surpassed any mode of transportation that had come before, and coaches soon became the rage of the fifteenth-century Europe . . . Over time, other forms of transportation adopted the term "coach." Passengers traveled the far reaches of the western frontier of America by stagecoach and railway coach . . . But however far-reaching and prevalent the word has become since the first coach rolled out of production in Kocs, the meaning has not changed. A "coach" remains something, or someone, who carries a valued person from where they are to where they want to be.[12]

From this definition, it's evident that coaches are transporters—physically and metaphorically—that can help us arrive at our desired destination. Over the years, I've had several coaches who have greatly influenced my life. One of them is Addison Bevere, who—since I moved to America—not only has been my boss at Messenger International but also a dear friend and coach. I am indebted to him and wouldn't be the person I am today without his involvement in my life. He's helped me grow as a man, leader, and writer. During the past five years in particular, he has poured himself into me, and from him I've gained insight into his thought processes, disciplines, and patterns of life.

One of the ways Addison has aided my growth is by helping me develop and implement a personal growth plan. Having this plan was a game-changer for me, and it involved Addison keeping me accountable every month to read a minimum of two books, listen to three podcasts, and work to complete at least three MasterClass courses a year.

Addison is also a brilliant writer whom I aspire to imitate. He's been intentional to coach me in this craft. Addison has helped transport me to level up as a person and writer—that's the value of a coach.

## The Apprentice

> When Jesus saw his ministry drawing huge crowds, he climbed a hillside. Those who were apprenticed to him, the committed, climbed with him. Arriving at a quiet place, he sat down and taught his climbing companions. (Matthew 5:1–2 MSG)

I love the choice of words used in The Message: "Those who were *apprenticed* to him . . . *climbed* with him," and "he sat down and taught his *climbing* companions." Mentors truly are like Sherpas; they guide us on our way up. We cannot ascend the upward journey without assistance from those who know the path and the "ropes."

Throughout Scripture, we come across examples of mentor–mentee relationships. Joshua was apprenticed to Moses. Elisha was apprenticed to Elijah. Ruth was apprenticed to Naomi. The disciples were apprenticed to Jesus. Timothy was apprenticed to Paul. And that's just the short list.

After a season of coaching and training from their mentors, each of these apprentices was released into the fullness of their God-given destiny. Most of them exceeded the accomplishments of their predecessors; their mentors' ceiling became their floor. On this topic, Jesus shared:

> "'Can a blind man guide a blind man?' Wouldn't they both end up in the ditch? An apprentice doesn't lecture the master. The point is to *be careful who you follow* as your teacher." (Luke 6:39–40 MSG)

Choosing mentors should be done carefully. Once you know your sphere of influence, then seek out a mentor from that sphere who can help you grow. If you're unable to work directly with or under them, find someone else who is a step or two ahead of you and learn from them. Set up meetings with them and come prepared to maximize your time together. In some cases, these mentors may have books or courses. If so, study them. Books make great mentors!

The apostle Paul gave us insight into effective apprenticeship when he wrote to Timothy:

> You've been a good apprentice to me, a part of my teaching, my manner of life, direction, faith, steadiness, love, patience, troubles, sufferings—suffering along with me in all the grief I had to put up with in Antioch, Iconium, and Lystra. And you also well know that God rescued me! Anyone who wants to live all out for Christ is in for a lot of trouble; there's no getting around it. Unscrupulous con men will continue to exploit the faith. They're as deceived as the people they lead astray. As long as they are out there, things can only get worse. (2 Timothy 3:10–13 MSG)

While being mentored by Paul, Timothy not only immersed himself in Paul's teachings, but also in his way of life, which included suffering.

When in 2004 I aligned my life with John Bevere, I began with immersing myself in his books and teachings, as well as volunteering to serve in his ministry in Sydney. This led to joining the team and working closely with John, which gave me the opportunity for direct coaching and mentoring. Having a front-row seat to John's life, I've witnessed him lead and navigate a variety of situations in which I could watch and learn.

Another man who has greatly impacted me is Phil Pringle, who was my pastor in Australia. During the years I served at C3 (Christian City Church), Phil poured himself into me and was instrumental in releasing me into ministry. Once a month for several years, Phil included me in an exclusive group of up-and-coming church leaders that he was mentoring in preaching and leadership. Those sessions helped awaken my gift of speaking and spurred my growth as a communicator. I also immersed myself in Phil's books and teachings.

What took Addison, John, and Phil years to learn and attain, I was receiving in a fraction of the time—all because of my alignment and proximity to them. That's the benefit of having a coach and a mentor.

### Circle of Influence

In addition to a mentor, the peers we surround ourselves with also can help us level up along our upward journey. I'm sure you've heard the saying, "Show me your friends and I'll show you your future." That's true because those closest to you will have the greatest influence on you. Solomon stated, "If you want to grow in wisdom, *spend time with the wise*. Walk with the wicked and *you'll eventually become just like them*" (Proverbs 13:20 TPT).

The fact is you become like those you spend the most time with. The company you surround yourself with is a reflection of your character and values. Whom you choose to associate with should be done with caution. For this reason, the Bible instructs, "The righteous should choose his friends carefully, for the way of the wicked leads them astray" (Proverbs 12:26).

Friend selection should not be taken lightly. Although it's common courtesy to be friendly toward everyone, you must not become friends with everyone. Again, the Word of God takes a strong stance on this matter: "The man of too many friends [chosen indiscriminately] will be broken in pieces and come to ruin" (Proverbs 18:24 AMP).

That's a stern warning! By no means does God's Word encourage an attitude of superiority toward others, because each of us is on a journey of growth and development. However, when it comes to associations, we are to be selective.

Consider again professional sports. I shared in Chapter Two my keen anticipation for the NBA draft every year. Draft day is an opportunity for teams to select players according to the needs and wants of the team. So much scouting, study, and consideration goes into draft choices, because the future of the organization is at stake.

Team owners and general managers will not only do their research, but they will also invest financially to assemble a team that can compete for, and even win, a championship. If the world of sports understands the importance of building a winning team, how much more important is it for you and me to surround ourselves with people who will help us win in life?

Your friend selections form the team that will direct the course of your future. And just like any good team has a variety of roles and positions, the people we associate with will play a variety of roles and positions in our life. And you will do the same for them.

Whether it's mentor–mentee or peer relationships, your life is greatly impacted—positively or negatively—by those closest to you. Although you cannot choose your family, coworkers, or even your neighbors, you can choose your friends. And according to God's Word, this should be done carefully.

## Helpful Criteria

What qualities should you look for when choosing friends? Here's a helpful list:

### Choose Friends You Enjoy

Nobody enjoys being around people they don't like. It's tiring and drains the life out of you. In regard to friends we enjoy, Solomon penned, "Just as lotions and fragrance give sensual delight, a sweet friendship refreshes the soul" (Proverbs 27:9 MSG).

A fundamental quality to look for in a friend is companionship—someone whose company you enjoy and they enjoy yours—celebrating you, not just tolerating you. The journey of life was never meant to be traveled alone. Surrounding yourself with friends you enjoy, and those who enjoy you, really makes a big difference and creates memories that will last a lifetime.

### Choose Friends Who Challenge You to Grow

Solomon wrote, "As iron sharpens iron, so one man sharpens [and influences] another [through discussion]" (Proverbs 27:17 AMP). People who challenge you to grow are themselves committed to personal growth. They are focused and disciplined and will hold you to a higher standard of conduct.

Friends who challenge you to grow also are truth-tellers. The Bible states:

> "Faithful are the wounds of a friend [who corrects out of love and concern], but the kisses of an enemy are deceitful [because they serve his hidden agenda]" (Proverbs 27:6 AMP).

As friends hold you accountable, you'll be motivated to live at your best.

### Choose Friends Who Are Trustworthy

A trusted friend is a confidant—one with whom you can confidentially and safely share a secret or private matter. Trust is both given and earned. As a friend proves themselves trustworthy, you can safely trust them with more. In the Bible, we are instructed:

"You can't trust gossipers with a secret; they'll just go blab it all. Put your confidence instead in a trusted friend, for he will be faithful to keep it in confidence" (Proverbs 11:13 TPT).

If you're surrounded by people who love to gossip and slander others, you can be sure they'll do the same to you behind your back. That's why we are warned not to associate with such people:

"He who goes about as a gossip reveals secrets; Therefore do not associate with a gossip [who talks freely or flatters]" (Proverbs 20:19 AMP).

Having a friend who sees the good and the bad, and yet remains loyal—such a friend is priceless!

*Choose Friends Who Share Your Values*
Associate with those who exhibit the qualities and values you hold and practice. Otherwise, you can eventually compromise your character. Even natural law concludes that more strength is required to pull something up than to pull something down. That's why the apostle Paul repeatedly warned, "Do not be deceived: 'Evil company corrupts good habits'" (1 Corinthians 15:33).

## Divine Connections

In 2008, as Messenger's Australian office managers were transitioning out, the ministry began looking to hire replacements. During the interviewing period, Messenger's CFO from the head office, Aaron, traveled to Sydney for a week to participate in the hiring process. Before Aaron arrived, the office manager, Esther, delegated specific days to each staff member to host Aaron while he was in town. When Esther had finished giving us all our instructions, she pulled me aside and prophesied to me, "Honor this man. He will play a huge role in your future!"

During the week Aaron was in town, an immediate bond grew between us. It felt like we had known each other our whole lives. In subsequent years, our friendship grew as we stayed in touch and took trips to visit each other. Looking back now, Aaron did play a huge part in my future, and he was pivotal in my move to America.

One of my favorite relationships recorded in the Bible, which exemplifies divine connection is between David and Jonathan. We're told:

> By the time David had finished reporting to Saul, Jonathan was deeply impressed with David—an immediate *bond* was forged between them. He became fully *committed* to David. From that point on he would be David's number-one *advocate* and friend.
> (1 Samuel 18:1 MSG)

When David and Jonathan crossed paths, an immediate bond was forged. From that point on, David and Jonathan would play significant roles in each other's life. Occasionally, you will experience a divine connection, a relationship divinely orchestrated by God to align you with your destiny. These relationships will impact your life like no other.

Sometimes, however, a divine connection may not translate into a close friendship. Occasionally, someone comes into our life for a reason and a season, to connect us to a new level of destiny. The ultimate purpose of a divine connection is to "link" you.

When Joseph was in prison in Egypt, God used the butler to link Joseph to Pharaoh. When Pharaoh was troubled by a dream, the butler remembered that two years earlier, when he was also imprisoned, Joseph had interpreted his dream. From one referral, Joseph was elevated from the prison to the palace.

This is similar to what David experienced. A young servant of King Saul was the link between David and Saul (see 1 Samuel 16). When Saul asked for a skilled musician, his servant recommended David. This brought David into the palace and caused him to level up toward his destiny.

Along your upward journey, be intentional about your relationships. Examine whether they help lift you up or hold you back. As you continue to grow and develop, not everyone will want to grow and develop with you. At a pivotal moment, you may have to go your separate ways, which means certain relationships will end while others will be embraced. The apostle Paul warned:

> *Stick with me,* friends. *Keep track of those you see running this same course,* headed for this same goal. There are many out there taking other paths, choosing other goals, and trying to get you to go along with them. I've warned you of them many times; sadly, I'm having to do it again. All they want is easy street. They hate Christ's Cross. But easy street is a dead-end street. Those who live there make their bellies their gods; belches are their praise; all they can think of is their appetites. (Philippians 3:17–19 MSG)

Look for those who are either running alongside you in the same direction or note those who are running up ahead of you. Both types of friends will help keep you on track. The upward path you're on is too important to be sidetracked by those who don't value where you want to end up.

## Pay It Forward

> So, my son, throw yourself into this work for Christ. Pass on what you heard from me . . . to reliable leaders who are competent to teach others. (2 Timothy 2:2 MSG)

The key phrase here is "pass on what you heard from me." The heart of what Paul is saying to Timothy is simply to do for others what Paul had done for him. In a nutshell, pay it forward!

Never lose sight of those who have helped you along the way. What would your life have looked like without their influence and involvement? Others are waiting for you to do the same for them. Who might you help along their upward journey? Consider Paul's words:

> Don't push your way to the front; don't sweet-talk your way to the top. Put yourself aside, and *help others get ahead*. Don't be obsessed with getting your own advantage. Forget yourselves long enough to *lend a helping hand*. (Philippians 2:3–4 MSG)

Don't miss what Paul said here. Helping others get ahead unlocks a spiritual principle: *What you make happen for others, God will make happen for you!* You'll reap what you sow. Therefore, you'll never lose when you put others first.

As you make your way up, be sure to reach a hand back to those who follow.

## CHEAT CODE

### Remember
- Our upward journey with God requires assistance from those with more experience.
- A mentor or coach is a "transporter"—someone who helps guide you from where you are to where you want to go.
- Who you hang out with matters. We become like those we associate with.
- Choose friends who are truth-tellers and trustworthy.
- Pay forward your wisdom and experience to others coming behind you.

### Reflect
1. How are you taking advantage of coaching to spur your "Leveling Up"? If you don't have a coach or mentor, who might become one for you?
2. How might you be a coach or mentor to others following you on the upward path?

# 10

# NEW LEVELS, NEW DEVILS

*The Higher You Go, the Greater the Resistance You'll Face*

Nothing of worth is ever accomplished without opposition. Whether that's starting a business, advancing in a karate tournament, or leveling up in a video game, the higher you go, the more difficult the opposition you'll encounter along the way.

By now you know of my love for sports, especially basketball—more specifically, NBA playoff basketball. During an eighty-two-game regular season, thirty teams compete for playoff spots. Once the regular season is over, the top eight teams from each conference (sixteen in total) advance to the playoffs in pursuit of a championship.

Advancing to the finals requires leveling up through the first, second, and conference final rounds. Then the winners of each conference go head-to-head in a best-of-seven series to win the Larry O'Brien Championship Trophy. Some of the best finals series are the nail-biters that go back and forth, reaching a climax in game seven. In these scenarios, the true warriors emerge, securing their athletic greatness.

After a champion is crowned, a documentary film is usually made chronicling the winning team's road to the finals. Even if my favorite team doesn't win, it's entertaining to watch the documentary that provides insight into the challenges, obstacles, and opposition the winning team had to overcome in order to win a championship. Knowing the whole story makes you appreciate their accomplishment even more. These films are a great reminder that the greater the battle, the greater the victory will be.

As we level up, we'll encounter a variety of opposing forces attempting to hold us back. Just like a sports team's road to the finals doesn't come without opponents, we, too, will face opposition from a rival, one who has hated "team Jesus" from the get-go. We are at war with the devil and his cohorts, who oppose anyone and everything that side with our Lord. Hear what the apostle Paul said on the topic:

> God is strong, and he wants you strong. So take everything the Master has set out for you, well-made weapons of the best materials. And put them to use so you will be able to stand up to everything the Devil throws your way. This is no weekend war that we'll walk away from and forget about in a couple of hours. This is for keeps, a life-or-death fight to the finish against the Devil and all his angels. (Ephesians 6:10–12 MSG)

This fight we're in is for real. Although this is a war, it's made up of many battles. Each battle will vary in intensity, especially when we go to new levels of destiny. This occurs because it's an opportunity for us to gain ground and occupy new territory, which threatens the enemy. That's why Paul also encouraged:

> But thanks be to God, who gives us the victory through our Lord Jesus Christ. Therefore, my beloved brethren, be steadfast, immovable, always abounding in the work of the Lord, knowing that your labor is not in vain in the Lord. (1 Corinthians 15:57–58)

Jesus has already given us the victory, but we are the ones who enforce it. That's why there are battles. The objective of opposition is to prevent us from progressing. Paul tells us that as we abound in God's work, we must remain steadfast and immovable. This means we must adopt an offensive posture and not back down from battle.

So, settle it in your heart right now: Your calling and purpose are worth fighting for.

## Opportunity Attracts Opposition

> A wide door for effective service has opened to me [in Ephesus, a very promising opportunity], and there are many adversaries.
> (1 Corinthians 16:9 AMP)

Opportunity attracts opposition, because the more important an action is to our destiny, the more resistance we'll experience. It's part and parcel with the territory—*new levels, new devils.*

According to *The Art of War* by Sun Tzu, an important rule of combat is to know your enemy. I'll illustrate this with another sports analogy. Whenever a team competes against another, especially in the playoffs, a game plan is developed to combat specifically the challenges from the opposing team. After studying the opposing team's offensive and defensive strategies, a game plan is created to give a team the best chance for winning.

Likewise, as we wage war against our enemy, we'll need to be aware of his strategies and devices in order to develop a winning game plan. What is a common tactic the enemy uses to prevent us from leveling up? Fear.

The pathway to your greatest potential often passes through your greatest fears. If you allow it, fear will hinder your destiny and rob your potential. Every time you decide to step out in faith or attempt something new, fear awaits, ready to hinder your progress or even stop you.

As a result of fear, the first generation of the children of Israel failed to possess the Promised Land. When the twelve spies returned from gathering intelligence on the Promised Land, ten gave a negative report that struck fear into the people. Although God had promised to give them the land and to fight on their behalf, the Israelites were still afraid.

Forty years later, after that first generation had passed away in the wilderness, it was time for the next generation to pick up where the first had left off. When Joshua was commissioned to lead Israel into the land, God said to him:

"This is my command—be strong and courageous! Do not be afraid or discouraged. For the LORD your God is with you wherever you go." (Joshua.1:9)

Notice that God "commanded" Joshua to be strong and courageous—a command God chose to repeat three times! Joshua had been part of that group of twelve spies who'd investigated the land forty years earlier. Only he and Caleb had been brave enough to want to take possession then, but they, too, had been made to wait until a whole generation had died.

So, I'm sure Joshua didn't need a reminder and was eager to lay hold of God's promise! But as a precaution, God made sure Joshua wouldn't allow fear to stop him from stepping up and stepping in. Joshua was strong and courageous and, eventually, did lead Israel to possess the land.

When we are in similar situations and must level up, we must also be strong and courageous. Courage is not the absence of fear; it's the choice to not allow fear to hold you back. Courage is taking action regardless of the feelings of fear. Ralph Waldo Emerson shared, "Fear defeats more people than any other one thing in the world."[13] And Mark Twain added, "Do the thing you fear, and the death of fear is certain."[14]

Throughout the Bible, we're repeatedly instructed to not fear. I used to think that this meant I could not "feel" afraid. Yet, through deeper study, I learned that the word *fear* actually means, "to flee" or "to take flight." Therefore, whenever the Lord says, "Fear not," He's not saying that we can't feel afraid; rather, He's telling us, "Don't let fear make you run!"

So, we see there are two responses to fear—fight or flight. Courage makes us fight; fear makes us flee!

The fear of public speaking had kept me bound for many years. When opportunities to teach and preach opened up for me, I had to face off with this fear. If I were to fulfill my calling as a teacher of God's Word, I would have to speak publicly.

The first time I preached in Australia, I remember sitting in the front row alongside my pastors. Several hundred people were in attendance, and I was gripped with fear. It was so bad that I couldn't engage in worship. My whole body trembled. Fearful thoughts ran through my mind. My mouth dried up. My stomach was full of butterflies. At one point, I thought I was about to puke the vegemite sandwich I'd eaten earlier. *I was much afraid!*

As the time to get up and preach drew closer, the feelings of fear grew stronger. Just before I almost ran out of the building, I took a few deep breaths and declared, "God is with me! I will not fear! I can do this!" I remember thinking, *If I don't face my fears now, I never will.*

I made the decision to get up and preach, regardless of how scared I felt. At that moment, I didn't care if I was laughed at or if I messed up. I knew that facing my fear and not running away was my victory.

That night, I preached my heart out. After a couple of minutes, I found my groove and never looked back. I discovered that I was more afraid before getting up to preach than while actually preaching. Fear is like that. It always appears scarier than it actually is. Do I still feel afraid before I get up to preach? Yes! It's just not as strong. The more I've faced my fears, the less fearful they have become to me.

Over the years, I've changed my perspective toward fear. Instead of viewing fear as opposition, I now view it as an opportunity. In his book *The War of Art*, Steven Pressfield wrote:

The more scared we are of a work or calling, the more sure we can be that we have to do it . . . Therefore the more fear we feel about a specific enterprise, the more certain we can be that that enterprise is important to us and to the growth of our soul. That's why we feel so much resistance.[15]

You'll never not experience fear. In your moments of fear, though, you can either view it as an opportunity or opposition, and how you respond will determine your outcome. Will you flee? Or fight? Again, the pathway to your greatest potential is often through your greatest fears.

In her book *A Return to Love*, Marianne Williamson shared:

Our deepest fear is not that we are inadequate. Our deepest fear is that we are powerful beyond measure. It is our light, not our darkness that most frightens us. We ask ourselves, "Who am I to be brilliant, gorgeous, talented, fabulous?" Actually, who are you not to be? You are a child of God. Your playing small does not serve the world. There is nothing enlightened about shrinking so that other people won't feel insecure around you. We are all meant to shine, as children do. We were born to make manifest the glory of God that is within us. It's not just in some of us; it's in everyone. And as we let our own light shine, we unconsciously give other people permission to do the same. As we are liberated from our own fear, our presence automatically liberates others.[16]

Your "playing small" does not serve the world. That's something I've had to remind myself often when facing fear. If you're dealing with fear now, you're not alone. We all encounter fear and you, too, can overcome it.

Looking back, I'm so thankful for the times I chose to face my fears.

Often, I did this intentionally—like choosing to sign up for a public speaking class. Each person was required to do a speaking exercise in front of the class every time we met. These exercises consisted of one- to two-minute impromptu speeches, five-minute planned speeches, and several other practical exercises.

As the weeks went by, I learned that most of my classmates were there not only to improve their public speaking skills, but even more so, to overcome their fears. I had the same goals, and after a few weeks, became more and more confident and courageous.

Whatever fear you're wrestling with, remember that your calling and purpose are worth fighting for.

Face your fears!

Let your light shine and make room for your true self to come forth!

Stir up your gifts!

The world needs what's inside of you!

## Protect Your Progress

> I press on to reach the end of the race and receive the heavenly prize for which God, through Christ Jesus, is calling us . . . But we must hold on to the progress we have already made. (Philippians 3:14, 16 NLT)

In order to keep making progress, half our battle will be protecting the progress we've already made. Not only are we contending to make progress; we're also contending to maintain it. The apostle John even warned us, "Be on your guard so that you do not lose all that we have *diligently* worked for but receive a full reward" (2 John 8 TPT).

Yes, hard-won progress can be lost.

I just shared how I had to face off with the fear of public speaking—and made definite progress. However, even now, if I've gone a while without any form of public speaking, I find myself slipping back into fear. So, to protect my progress, I find ways of standing my ground.

A helpful exercise I do involves using my imagination. In a quiet place, I close my eyes and picture myself standing in front of an audience. I try to think of every detail—people's faces staring at me, the auditorium, the atmosphere. I "see" myself holding the crowd's attention—they are so rapt that the people are affirming my words by taking plenty of notes.

When I do this, it feels so real, like I'm actually in front of a crowd. This exercise helps train my subconscious mind, so when I actually do speak to an audience, it feels like I've done it so many times already that there's not much of a fear-inducing shock.

Another way to protect your progress is to avoid things that hinder it. This reminds me of a board game I used to play during my childhood with my parents called "Snakes and Ladders" (also known as "Chutes and Ladders"). The game was originally designed to teach children morality lessons: a player's progression up the board represented a life journey impacted by virtues (ladders) and vices (snakes).

It's a simple game played on a board with gridded squares. A variety of "ladders" and "snakes" are pictured on the board. The head and tail of each snake connect board squares, and likewise for the bottom and top of the ladders. If your game piece lands on a snake's head, you are moved down to the tail of the snake. If your piece lands on the foot of the ladder, you are moved up.

The object of the game is to navigate one's game piece, according to die rolls, from the start to the finish. How fast or slowly you move through the game is helped by the ladders or hindered by the snakes.

Now that I'm a parent, I love playing this game with my son. It's a good opportunity for us to bond and to teach him some life lessons. The analogies that can be drawn from snakes and ladders are many, but an obvious one is that along our upward journey, we should avoid those things that hinder our progress and look for the things that accelerate it. How can we do this?

## Stay Focused

While we navigate our way forward, our focus must remain on our mission, not on our opposition. Thereby, our mission itself provides motivation to resist our opposition.

> Set your gaze on the path before you. With fixed purpose, looking straight ahead, *ignore life's distractions*. (Proverbs 4:25 TPT)

Opposition can become a distraction. If left unaddressed, it will break your focus and hinder your progress.

Clyde Beaty, a well-known lion tamer, is famous for his use of a chair to tame a lion. Whenever he would enter a cage with a lion, he brought with him three items: a gun, a whip, and a chair. If that were me entering that cage, I'd feel somewhat safe with a gun or a whip, but a chair? I don't think so!

But Clyde understood that lions are very focused and single-minded creatures. To tame the lion, he'd have to break its focus. When using the chair, he knew that the lion wasn't intimidated by it but, rather, confused. Whenever the lion would make a move toward him, Clyde would hold up the chair to its face, causing the lion to back off. The chair was effective because the four points of its legs distracted the lion, breaking its focus. And with its focus diverted, the lion was paralyzed and more easily tamed.

This story depicts the power of distraction and how it can immobilize us. Once your focus is broken, it's easier to lose sight of where you're headed and how far you've come. That's why we must diligently focus on our purpose. Where our focus goes, our energy flows. Paul shared, "Therefore I do not run uncertainly (without definite aim). I do not box like one beating the air *and* striking without an adversary" (1 Corinthians 9:26 AMPC).

Paul said he ran with "definite aim," which means his goal was clear. When your purpose is clear, you are empowered to know what to say "yes" to and what to say "no" to.

## Stretch Your Faith

Our faith stretches every time we advance to a new level. According to Scripture, "faith *brings our hopes into reality* and becomes the foundation needed to acquire the things we long for" (Hebrews 11:1 TPT). When stretching our faith, we reach for a future reality and pull it into the present.

Paul shared that God has given each of us a "measure" of faith (Romans 12:3). And throughout the New Testament, we see a variety of faith levels ranging from no faith (Mark 4:40), to little faith (Matthew 6:30; Matthew 16:8), all the way to great faith (Matthew 8:10; Matthew 15:28). You don't need to worry about your level of faith. Whether you have little faith or great faith, the good news is that your faith can grow and increase (Romans 10:17; 2 Corinthians 10:15).

Often during the disciples' time with Jesus, He blew their minds with what He said and did. Like the time Jesus discussed the importance of forgiveness and how the disciples were to extend mercy. Upon hearing this, they said, "Lord, you must increase our measure of faith!" (Luke 17:5 TPT). The truth that they were attempting to comprehend, which would position them for a new level of growth, required their faith to be stretched and increased.

To answer their request, Jesus used an example of the way in which a servant's work in the field or with their livestock isn't complete the moment they quit for the day. It's only when servants make sure their master is fed—that's when they've completed their duties:

> "So learn this lesson: After doing all that is commanded of you, simply say, 'We are mere servants, undeserving of special praise, for we are just doing what is expected of us and fulfilling our duties.'" (Luke 17:10 TPT)

Our faith grows as we obey the task to completion. Faith is increased through obedience to God.

With this understanding, we see that faith is more than a means to receive answers from God; it also empowers us to live in God—"the just shall live by faith" (Romans 1:17). As we carry out our assignments, we must obey to completion so that we can advance to new levels and increase our faith. Faith, therefore, is like a muscle that grows through exercise. The more we use it, the more its strength increases.

The stretching of your faith could look like believing God for greater influence, more resources, more clients, scaling your business, fundraising, buildings, and other facilities—and yes, even overcoming the fear of public speaking.

## Get Back Up

No one journeys through life perfectly. Life throws punches that can ground us. When we fall, we can choose to stay down or get back up. In the words of screen boxer Rocky Balboa:

> "The world ain't all sunshine and rainbows. It's a very mean and nasty place and I don't care how tough you are, it will beat you to your knees and keep you there permanently if you let it. You, me, or nobody is gonna hit as hard as life. But it ain't about how hard ya hit. It's about how hard you can get hit and keep moving forward. How much you can take and keep moving forward. That's how winning is done!"[17]

The distinguishing factor between winners and losers is that winners keep getting back up. They roll with the punches and keep moving forward—even if it means an inch at a time. The Bible says:

> For the lovers of God may suffer adversity and stumble seven times, but *they will continue to rise over and over again*. But the unrighteous are brought down by just one calamity and will never be able to rise again. (Proverbs 24:16 TPT)

Over a decade ago, while living in Australia, my pastors introduced me to a girl (I'll call her Melissa). She was a close friend to them and often babysat their children. My pastors were always trying to play Cupid, and this time Melissa and I were their target. The moment I met Melissa, I had a check in my spirit—something didn't feel right about her.

She was a very attractive girl and "ticked a lot of boxes." She was attending church, fit, healthy, a dancer. But I sensed she was living a double life—behaving one way at church and another outside of it. For a whole year they tried to set us up, but I kept resisting. I knew in my heart it wasn't the right thing to do.

On one occasion, while meeting privately with my pastors, they sternly got on my case for how I was missing God's will for my life by refusing to date Melissa. I was even rebuked for being critical and judgmental of her, although I knew God was telling me not to get involved with her. I wanted to honor my pastors, so I began dating her.

After several months of dating, Melissa's true colors emerged. But by that time, though, I'd fallen in love with her. I overlooked several red flags so as not to be "critical" or "judgmental." Looking back, I should've ended the relationship, regardless of what my pastors thought. But I stuck around too long. And, eventually, I succumbed to temptation and compromised my values.

Soon after, I confessed my shortcomings to these pastors, and they were gracious with me. I stepped down for a few months from any form of ministry to rest and heal. At first, this caused me to sink into depression, guilt, and shame—I had no one else to blame but myself.

I was angry that I'd chosen to please man over God. I was disappointed that I didn't set healthy boundaries and had ignored the warnings. The regret was overwhelming because I should've known better.

Although I'd fallen, I knew I had to get back up again. I was sinking and needed to hold on to hope. It wasn't easy, and I often wrestled with thoughts that I'd ruined God's call on my life. Thankfully, I'm not that powerful! I took ownership for my mistakes and remained planted at church—even though I wanted to run.

In many ways, I'm thankful I was able to deal with my issues on a much lower level rather than later in life when consequences could've been a lot worse. During this time of rest, I drew closer to God and experienced a lot of inner healing. Areas of brokenness, pride, and selfishness were exposed, and God did a deep work in my heart. He was very gracious to me, and I experienced His love in a way I had not known before.

A few months later, I met with my pastors again. This time, the meeting was different. They apologized for trying to force me to marry Melissa. They also shared how proud they were of the way I'd chosen to handle the situation. My relationship with them was healed, and I was reinstated to ministry.

As I reflect on that season, I'm thankful I chose not to stay down too long. My life would look totally different today if I had not gotten back up. What I initially thought was a setback actually became a setup for greater fruitfulness.

God is redemptive. Even though everything that happens may be our fault, when we genuinely repent, He'll always shower us with mercy and grace. And not only that, but what the enemy meant for evil, He will turn around for our good—if we'll allow Him to do so.

It doesn't matter if your fall was your fault. God can create miracles from your mistakes. When you stumble and fall, get back up! Whether it's a moral failure, a bankruptcy, a breakup or divorce, a season-ending injury, a loss of a job or a loved one—don't give up! Dust yourself off and keep moving forward. It might take time to get back on your feet, but before you know it, you'll hit the ground running again.

## Stay Hungry

A hunger to fulfill your purpose will protect you from coasting through life and settling for less than God's best. Once you've reached a level of success that you think is good enough, it's easy to become complacent and lose motivation. But those who desire all that God has for them will remain hungry for it.

Life motivation comes from the deep longings of the heart, and the passion to see them fulfilled urges you onward. (Proverbs 16:26 TPT)

As we've already discussed, Caleb and Joshua had to wait forty years—until they were older men—before they could once again set foot in the Promised Land. During those four decades of wandering in the desert, I'm sure Caleb and Joshua had several opportunities to complain, lose hope, and grow complacent.

Yet they remained hungry. They had seen a glimpse of what was to come, and they refused to settle for anything less. This is evident in Caleb's words to Joshua, as he was assigning portions of land among the children of Israel:

> Then the children of Judah came to Joshua in Gilgal. And Caleb the son of Jephunneh the Kenizzite said to him: "You know the word which the LORD said to Moses the man of God concerning you and me in Kadesh Barnea. I was forty years old when Moses the servant of the LORD sent me from Kadesh Barnea to spy out the land, and I brought back word to him as it was in my heart. Nevertheless my brethren who went up with me made the heart of the people melt, but I wholly followed the LORD my God. So Moses swore on that day, saying, 'Surely the land where your foot has trodden shall be your inheritance and your children's forever, because you have wholly followed the LORD my God.'
> 
> And now, behold, the LORD has kept me alive, as He said, these forty-five years, ever since the LORD spoke this word to Moses while Israel wandered in the wilderness; and now, here I am this day, eighty-five years old. As yet I am as strong this day as on the day that Moses sent me; just as my strength was then, so now is my strength for war, both for going out and for coming in. Now therefore, give me this mountain of which the LORD spoke in that day; for you heard in that day how the Anakim were there,

and that the cities were great and fortified. It may be that the LORD will be with me, and I shall be able to drive them out as the LORD said." And Joshua blessed him, and gave Hebron to Caleb the son of Jephunneh as an inheritance. (Joshua 14:6–13)

As you read this account, did you capture the passion in Caleb's words? After holding onto God's promise for more than forty years, he declared, "Now, therefore, give me this mountain!" That's a man who'd remained hungry for all that God had purposed for him. That's the same tenacity we must have to lay hold of all that God has purposed for us also.

Delay is not denial. Delays often reveal how much we really want something. If we give up too soon, did we really want it? But hunger will continue to fuel our upward journey.

My friend, stay hungry.

## The Benefits of Opposition

"The impediment to action advances action. What stands in the way becomes the way."—Marcus Aurelius

Opposition creates opportunity. I believe opposition awakens a fight within our inner person that cannot be awakened without it. In that awakening, we discover strength we didn't know we had.

I immediately think of David confronting Goliath. While the rest of the children of Israel were hiding in fear, Goliath revealed the fighter in David. What was in David came forth as a result of opposition. By God's grace, David was transformed from a lowly shepherd boy to a valiant man of war. And from that opposition came great opportunity.

This victory gave David much-needed exposure and, in many ways, was catalytic for his ascent to the throne. What stood in the way (Goliath) became the way.

In his book *David and Goliath*, author Malcolm Gladwell shared:

> Being an underdog can change people in ways that we often fail to appreciate: it can open doors and create opportunities and educate and enlighten and make possible what might otherwise have seemed unthinkable.[18]

Many pivotal moments in my life have come as a result of feeling like an underdog. The fighter within refuses to accept defeat or denial. I'm not sure what it really is, but perhaps it's that eternity in our heart nudging us toward greater growth. Whatever the explanation, I'm sure it's God's way of letting us know we were made for more.

In light of this, my spiritual mom, Lisa Bevere, has often said, "A rival can either best you or bring out the best in you." I couldn't agree more.

My prayer for you is that an opposing rival will bring out the best in you.

Another aspect about sports that I love is the rivalries that develop over the years between players and teams. When these players and teams go against each other, it's fun to watch them up their game. These rivalries have created memorable moments in sports history. That's the power of having a rival. If handled correctly, they'll bring out the best in you—and even some things you didn't know were in you!

The apostle Paul also had to learn this lesson. He wrote:

> The extraordinary level of the revelations I've received is no reason for anyone to exalt me. For this is why a thorn in my flesh was given to me, the Adversary's messenger sent to harass me, keeping me from becoming arrogant. (2 Corinthians 12:7 TPT)

Paul had an opponent sent from Satan to harass him. This could be the reason why Paul constantly fought battles everywhere he went. At first, Paul viewed his opposition as a threat to his purpose. In a desperate cry for relief, three times he pleaded with the Lord to deliver him from these attacks. But Jesus's response is very interesting:

But he answered me, "My grace is always more than enough for you, and my power finds its full expression through your weakness." So I will celebrate my weaknesses, for when I'm weak I sense more deeply the mighty power of Christ living in me. (2 Corinthians 12:9–10 TPT)

To paraphrase, Jesus was saying, "The opposition you're experiencing is an opportunity to experience my power in a way you've never experienced before. Having an adversary allows you to enforce the victory I've already won for you!"

Paul's perspective toward opposition changed, and he no longer saw these attacks as setbacks; he began to see them as a setup—an opportunity for God to show Himself strong to him and through him. That's also the attitude we must possess toward opposition.

Are you pleading with God to remove what He desires for you to confront?

---

As we continue on our upward journey, we'll encounter opposition. With new levels comes new devils. But as we saw with David and Paul—what stands in the way becomes the way.

Fight for your destiny and protect your progress. Stay focused, stretch your faith, stay hungry, and if you fall, get right back up!

## CHEAT CODE

### Remember
- Nothing worth accomplishing comes without opposition.
- We are in a spiritual war: Jesus has won the victory, but we must enforce it.
- "The pathway to your greatest potential often passes through your greatest fears."
- Progress in the Christian life must be protected.
- Never lose sight of your aim.
- Opposition can bring out your best.

### Reflect
1. What opposition to your spiritual progress are you facing now? How might you respond?
2. Are you stuck because of a failure or unresolved guilt or shame? What's preventing you—with God's forgiveness—from moving forward?

# 11

# PRAYER, POWER, AND BREAKTHROUGH

*Spiritual Victories Precede Physical Ones*

Early in my walk with God, I wrestled with understanding the purpose and power of prayer. Not that I didn't believe prayer was powerful! It was the fact that the religion I grew up in made prayer appear boring and mundane.

During those early days of walking with the Lord, He spoke to me through a vision that invigorated my prayer life and brought much-needed understanding about this wonderful weapon of war—especially the importance of praying in tongues.

In the vision, I stood with a two-edged sword in my hand, in front of a field of tall, thick, green grass. As I prayed in tongues, I saw myself slicing through the thick grass, creating a pathway. Periodically, dark figures would appear. I would stab them with my sword, and they would instantly disintegrate. This happened several times until I finally cut my way through the thick grass into a wide-open, spacious field.

Immediately, I heard the Holy Spirit say, "This is what happens when you pray in tongues. You're praying into your future, paving a way for yourself to step into your destiny, while winning future battles in the spirit along the way."

After this vision, my perspective toward praying in tongues instantly changed—I realized that this type of prayer was more than receiving from God; it was warfare! Through praying in tongues, I could break through spiritual opposition and step into my God-given destiny. Aided by God's Spirit, I was praying the perfect will of God for myself.

## Breakthrough

The idea of a "breakthrough" reveals many facets of leveling up.

*Breakthrough in regard to opposition* is when we take ground from or enter enemy-occupied territory. This can occur physically, such as on June 6, 1944, when 156,000 troops made up of Allied Forces from Britain, France, Canada, and the United States attacked German forces on the coast of Normandy, France. This effort gained a victory that was pivotal in World War II. This type of breakthrough can also occur spiritually, such as in the vision that I described.

*Another type of breakthrough can occur with an obstacle.* Examples would be the breakthrough that ended slavery or an improvement in one's health or finances. It could also refer to answers to prayer and the removal of people and situations standing in the way of fulfilling your God-given destiny.

*Still another breakthrough would be a new and revolutionary idea, product, or practice.* This can be in relation to a medical breakthrough, a technological advancement, or a new way to get rock-hard abs!

*A final kind of breakthrough would be a person's first notable success or triumph.* This could be a book that becomes a bestseller—launching an author's literary success, an actress's award-winning performance, or the seizing of a life-defining opportunity.

All these types of breakthroughs reveal how necessary they are to leveling up. They provide a sudden leap, boost, or advancement into our destiny. Throughout our upward journey, God will use breakthroughs to accelerate His plans and purposes in which He opens the way for yourself or others to reach further and achieve more. What was once our ceiling now becomes our floor.

Breakthroughs appear throughout Scripture and are a defining attribute of God. For example, in 2 Samuel 5:20, the Lord gave David victory over the Philistines: "The LORD has broken through my enemies before me, like a breakthrough of water."

So, accordingly, David named the place *Baal-perazim*, which means "master of breakthroughs." Before David's victory, this place was called the Valley of Rephaim, which meant "house of the giant." For us, in a similar way, the places where giants stand in opposition to us will become the places in which God establishes His breakthroughs! Nothing can stand in the way of our God!

David contrasted the working of God to a breakthrough of water. Another translation says, "He burst through my enemies like a raging flood" (NLT). Water is a powerful force! Floods and tsunamis leave destruction in their wake. Whole villages and even nations have been flattened to ruins by the force of these waters. They give us a graphic illustration of how, when God breaks through, there's no stopping Him.

In another Scripture we read:

> From the west to the lands of the rising sun, the glory and the name of Yahweh will be held in highest reverence, for he will break in as a flooding, rushing river driven on by the breath of Yahweh! (Isaiah 59:19 TPT)

Once again, we see the breakthrough nature of our God, this time as a rushing river.

Nowhere is this truth more evident than in Jesus's victory on the cross! His completed work broke open a new way of life, liberating mankind from the bondage of evil:

> The breaker [the Messiah, who opens the way] shall go up before them [liberating them]. They will break out, pass through the

gate and go out; So their King goes on before them, The LORD at their head. (Micah 2:13 AMP)

At the cross, Jesus defeated the enemy and broke the human race free from Satan's rule and power—and brought with Him those the devil had held captive. He opened the way for us to know salvation, freedom, and our identity as sons and daughters of God, while reconciling us back to the loving embrace of our heavenly Father.

On top of all that, it was a defining moment for Jesus as He became the first to be raised from the dead as a glorified man (see 1 Corinthians 15:20–28). He became the "first fruits" of what we shall become when we conquer death and receive our final salvation. This is why the gospel is so important! Paul wrote, "For the message of the cross is foolishness to those who are perishing, but to us who are being saved *it is the power of God"* (1 Corinthians 1:18).

Breakthrough comes to us the moment we believe the good news of what Jesus has done for us!

## Breakthrough Prayer

As believers, we can continue to experience breakthroughs as we partner with Jesus in prayer. It doesn't stop at conversion—we can continue to experience breakthroughs when we partner with God to advance His kingdom on the earth. Jesus taught, "'Repent, for the kingdom of heaven is *at hand,*'" (Matthew 4:17).

The phrase "at hand" in the Greek language carries the idea of a tidal wave ready to crash in. This means that the kingdom of heaven is ready to breakthrough like a tidal wave! "At hand" also means that the kingdom is accessible and within reach. We've already discussed how the kingdom must be sought after with ardent zeal and intense exertion:

> And from the days of John the Baptist until the present time, the kingdom of heaven has endured violent assault, and violent

men seize it by force [as a precious prize—a share in the heavenly kingdom is sought with the most ardent zeal and intense exertion]. (Matthew 11:12 AMPC)

Once again, I want to highlight the words "violent assault," "seize by force," and "precious prize." When we approach prayer with this kind of tenacity, we'll see God's kingdom break through here on earth.

In Matthew 15:21–28, a Gentile woman's hunger and persistence for her daughter's miracle caused her to access, in her day, what was reserved for a future time. After several attempts to get the attention of Jesus and His disciples, her breakthrough came as she persisted and became more aggressive in faith. Jesus responded, and the woman went home that day and found her daughter completely healed!

So far, we've seen God's breakthroughs described as a rushing flood, a raging river, and a tidal wave. Staying with our water theme, the analogy of rain offers another breakthrough perspective: "When clouds are heavy, the rains come down" (Ecclesiastes 11:3 NLT).

A rain cloud accumulates water gradually until it cannot contain the weight of the moisture, and then the water pours out upon the earth. There's a buildup, and then a release. The same applies to prayer. The more our prayers build momentum, the more power will be released.

The correlation between rain and prayer is very interesting. Rain clouds are formed by a four-step process that includes evaporation, condensation, saturation, and precipitation.

How is this like prayer? Breakthrough prayer involves a collecting of passionate and persistent intercession. The more we pray (evaporation), the more power that is formed (saturation and condensation), which ultimately leads to a breaking point (precipitation)—the releasing of answers and provisions we've asked for.

Throughout the Bible, rain is symbolic of God's blessing, favor, and provision. It's also a symbol of His Spirit and His presence (see Joel 2:28–29; Acts 2:17–18). Here are a few samples:

Your favor will fall like rain upon our surrendered lives, like showers reviving the earth. (Psalm 72:6 TPT)

Let us know, let us pursue the knowledge of the LORD. His going forth is established as the morning; He will come to us like the rain, like the latter *and* former rain to the earth. (Hosea 6:3)

In the light of the king's face *is* life, and his favor *is* like a cloud of the latter rain. (Proverbs 16:15)

Leveling up into God's plans and purposes for your life will require persistent prayer. As you do this, you'll see a breakthrough of blessing, favor, provision, and God's power displayed in miraculous ways. Certain doors and pathways will open up to you. Certain battles will be fought and won.

Keep chipping away in prayer. Sooner or later, you'll see a breakthrough!

I find it interesting that the one thing we know for sure that Jesus's disciples asked Him to teach them was *how to pray* (see Luke 11:1). They lived and worked with Jesus for three years. They saw Him outsmart those who were considered wise. They saw Him perform miracles, heal the sick, raise the dead, and cast out demons. Yet, it's not recorded that they ever asked Him to teach them how to do those things. They knew Jesus's works were a result of His prayer life. This is why they wanted to be taught how to pray.

Knowing how to pray, therefore, is the key to spiritual breakthroughs. Let's take a closer look at what God's Word tells us about praying effectively.

## Persistent Prayer

The heartfelt *and* persistent prayer of a righteous man (believer) can accomplish much [when put into action and made effective by God—it is dynamic and can have tremendous power]. (James 5:16 AMP)

The prayers that matter to God are the ones that originate from the depths of our heart. These are the genuine, no-holds-barred prayers that please God. Heartfelt prayers are passionate and powerful. They're not done by religious rote or obligation; they're the cries of a desperate heart.

When you couple those prayers with persistence, then you have a recipe for breakthrough! To "persist" in prayer is to do so resolutely or stubbornly in spite of opposition, delay, or circumstance. Here's how Jesus explained the power of persistent prayer:

> Then Jesus gave this illustration: "Imagine what would happen if you were to go to one of your friends in the middle of the night and pound on his door and shout, 'Please! Do you have some food you can spare? A friend just arrived at my house unexpectedly and I have nothing to serve him.' But your friend says, 'Why are you bothering me? The door is locked and my family and I are all in bed. Do you expect me to get up and give you our food?'
>
> But listen—because of your shameless impudence, even though it's the middle of the night, your friend will get up out of his bed and give you all that you need. So it is with your prayers. Ask and you'll receive. Seek and you'll discover. Knock on heaven's door, and it will one day open for you. Every persistent person will get what he asks for. Every persistent seeker will discover what he needs. And everyone who knocks persistently will one day find an open door. (Luke 11:5–10 TPT)

A few things stand out in this story. The first is not the fact that the person knocking got his request—it's how he got it! At any other time, the friend would've given to him what he asked for. But persistence got his request when it normally would have been ignored.

When we persist in heartfelt prayer, the things we're asking for will happen faster than they would otherwise—because of the power that accumulates. The late E.M. Bounds shared:

> "Prayer puts God in the matter with commanding force. The secret of prayer and its success lie in its urgency. We must press our prayers upon God."[19]

Another factor in the parable is that the person persisting with his friend did so on behalf of someone else. The friend had a friend who'd come to town unexpectedly and needed food and a place to stay. The guy being shamelessly persistent had a righteous motive! When we cry out to God on behalf of others, especially as it pertains to our individual calling, God takes note!

God will trust us with greater breakthroughs when our heart desires to help others.

The final thing I want to point out about persistent prayers is that they're determined prayers. A person praying persistent prayers refuses to accept no for an answer. That's why Jesus said that every persistent person will get what they ask for. If you don't want it badly enough, you'll quit asking. But someone who's determined won't stop knocking until the door comes crashing down. You can do this, too, by persisting in prayer.

## Prayer and Fasting

All through Scripture you'll find that the people and nations who wanted to experience a breakthrough fasted and prayed. In fact, when Jesus taught on prayer, He also taught on fasting. In the same passage in which Jesus says, "When you pray" (Matthew 6:5–7), not, "If you pray." He also says, "When you fast" (Matthew 6:16–17), not, "If you fast."

In many ways, just as prayer is non-negotiable so, too, is fasting. We can pray without fasting, but we should never fast without praying. That's because fasting should not be reduced to a weight-loss method; it's a spiritual discipline that provides a variety of spiritual benefits.

On one occasion, as the disciples were ministering to others, they had trouble casting out a particular demon. In response, Jesus shared, "this kind is cast out only through prayer and fasting" (Matthew 17:21 TPT).

So, we see clearly that in order for prayer to be effective, it had to be combined with fasting—then the breakthrough occurred.

Another example of the power of prayer and fasting is when the prophet Daniel had been seeking God for an answer for twenty-one days through prayer while fasting. Finally, after the three weeks, Daniel had a spiritual breakthrough. His encounter with an angel explains a lot about the nature of the spirit realm, as well as the influence that prayer and fasting have there:

> Then he said to me, "Do not fear, Daniel, for from the first day that you set your heart to understand, and to humble yourself before your God, your words were heard; and I have come because of your words. But the prince of the kingdom of Persia withstood me twenty-one days; and behold, Michael, one of the chief princes, came to help me, for I had been left alone there with the kings of Persia. Now I have come to make you understand what will happen to your people in the latter days, for the vision *refers* to *many* days yet *to come* . . .
>
> Then he said, "Do you know why I have come to you? And now I must return to fight with the prince of Persia; and when I have gone forth, indeed the prince of Greece will come. But I will tell you what is noted in the Scripture of Truth. (No one upholds me against these, except Michael your prince.)" (Daniel 10:12–14, 20–21)

Notice that from the first day Daniel set his heart to seek the Lord, his prayers were heard. Yet, we see that it took twenty-one days of fasting and prayer to receive a breakthrough. During that time, a battle waged between God's angel and a demon principality named the Prince of Persia. Once the battle ended, the angel could deliver his message. This account reveals why sometimes our prayers are delayed or hindered.

When we fast and pray, spiritual warfare and angelic activity take place on our behalf, opening the way for God's answers to flow unhindered. In response to our prayers and fasting, God dispatches angels and begins to release His breakthrough.

In both examples I've listed, a strongman spirit was involved that could only be dealt with correctly by prayer and fasting.

### Bind the Strongman

> For who is powerful enough to enter the house of a strong man and plunder his goods? Only someone even stronger—someone who could tie him up and then plunder his house. (Matthew 12:29 NLT)

These words Jesus spoke reveal what He actually did to Satan. Through the cross, Jesus . . .

> canceled out every legal violation we had on our record and the old arrest warrant that stood to indict us. He erased it all—our sins, our stained soul—he deleted it all *and they cannot be retrieved!* . . . Then Jesus made a public spectacle of all the powers and principalities of darkness, stripping away from them every weapon and all their spiritual authority and power to accuse us. And by the power of the cross, Jesus led them around as prisoners in a procession of triumph. *He was not their prisoner; they were his!*" (Colossians 2:14–15 TPT).

Satan once had a stronghold on humanity, but Jesus stripped the devil of his power and secured victory for all who believe on His name. The apostle John wrote:

> "The reason the Son of God was made manifest (visible) was to undo (destroy, loosen, and dissolve) the works the devil [has done]" (1 John 3:8 AMPC).

Now, as believers, whenever we engage in spiritual warfare and apply our God-given authority, we invoke the Lord's victory, continuing to undo the works of the devil in the lives of others.

One of the ways we do this is by binding the strongman spirit over people, cities, and nations. In his book, *You the Leader*, Pastor Phil Pringle shares an account with a strongman spirit that had been assigned to hinder the progress of his church. During the 1980s, Phil had repeatedly attempted to secure rezoning of a large piece of land to build a church sanctuary. For seven years, he had encountered opposition from the local government, residents, and media outlets. On top of that, he'd frequently received late-night phone calls from Satanists screaming and gurgling on the other end of the line.

A breakthrough moment came in 1989 during the church's annual faith conference. While Pastor Phil sat in the front row, he became aware of a demon crouching before him in a ready-to-pounce stance. He described the demon as strong and muscular, having its eyes firmly fixed on him. Several times under his breath, he told the demon to leave, but nothing happened.

During the conference, the guest speaker was teaching on the power of God's Word, and immediately Pastor Phil made the connection. In that moment, the Holy Spirit quickened Romans 8:28 to Phil and he began to speak it out, but this time, with more authority. As he did so, the demon sneezed, wiped its nose, and then stared right back at him, resuming its stance.

During that encounter, Pastor Phil realized that this strongman spirit had been devoted to opposing him on the property for the new church building. After the service, Phil went straight to his room to pray. While praying, he once again saw a vision of the demon, except this time it appeared smaller, weaker, and further away. Phil continued to pray and, eventually, sensed the battle was won.

The Lord then spoke to him, saying, "The devil is bound. You have a clear run to the end." After these words, Phil saw the demon bound with chains, trying without success to break loose.

Within a few weeks, the local government approved plans for construction and building was underway, unopposed by anyone—including the Satanists! In fact, not only did the church receive funding from the state, but Muslim contractors also offered their services at cost—saving Phil's church thousands of dollars!

Since then, from this location, Pastor Phil has led thousands to the Lord, hundreds of missionaries and church planters have been sent out, and thousands of Bible college students have been trained, equipped, and released to do ministry. All of this—after binding the strongman spirit.[20]

As believers, we have the same power and authority that Jesus had (see Matthew 28:18–20 and Ephesians 2:6). As you will recall from Chapter Three, we looked at how we're seated with Christ in heavenly places, and we can live from that higher realm.

That means, like Christ, we have the advantage and hold a position of strength. From that heavenly place, we have the authority to bind and overcome the devil, plundering his goods. And because of our prayers, we can release God's power and authority here on earth. Jesus taught:

> Listen to the truth I speak to you: If someone says to this mountain with great faith and having no doubt, "Mountain, be lifted up and thrown into the midst of the sea," and believes that what he says will happen, it will be done. (Mark 11:23 TPT)

Prayer is more than *asking*; it's also *declaring*. When we stand in the place of Christ on the earth, as His body and representatives, we release His authority and kingdom rule here. As we do this, mountains are leveled, obstacles are removed, and the impossible is made possible.

The footnotes from *The Passion Translation* share more clarity:

1. Mark 11:23: The Aramaic word for *doubt* means "to be divided (undecided) in your heart."
2. Mark 11:23: The mountain and the sea can also be metaphors. Mountains in the Bible can refer to kingdoms, and the sea represents the nations (e.g., "sea of humanity"). Faith lifts up and brings with us the "mountain" of God's kingdom realm when we go into the nations. The Greek word for mountain, *oros*, is related to a verb that means "to lift up and carry off and take with you." This truth Jesus brings us is more than hyperbole; it is the active power of faith to take and carry the power and authority of the mountain—God's kingdom realm—with us wherever we go.

Notice that our words have power. Jesus said, "Whoever *says* to this mountain." He does not say, "Those who *ask* for the mountain to be removed." Faith believes in the heart and speaks with the mouth! Just like Pastor Phil had to speak to the strongman demon and exercise his God-given authority, we too must also speak to our mountains, exercising our faith and our God-given authority.

Once we do, we'll also see mountains leveled, obstacles removed, and victory enforced over demonic foes. In the name of Jesus, *every* knee shall bow, especially those of demons:

> "Everything and everyone will one day submit to this name—in the heavenly realm, in the earthly realm, and *in the demonic realm.*" (Philippians 2:10 TPT)

You can break through any obstacle by the power of prayer. Allow the Holy Spirit to lead and guide you. He'll teach and show you what you need to pray against.

*With the help of God's Spirit, nothing and no one can stand in your way.*

What areas of your life have seemed to remain unchanged?

What battles have continued without resolution?

What doors have remained shut?

It's time for you to go to war in prayer!

### Pray in the Spirit

The gift of tongues is a greatly underrated gift in the Body of Christ. If we could grasp the power produced by this form of prayer, we'd never question its validity again. The New Testament identifies four types of tongues: tongues for personal edification, tongues for interpretation (which becomes prophecy), tongues as a sign to unbelievers, and tongues for intercession.

For the purpose of this chapter, I want to discuss tongues for intercession. (If you'd like to learn more about the gift of tongues, I encourage you to read John Bevere's book *The Holy Spirit: An Introduction*). Paul prayed in tongues more than anyone (see 1 Corinthians 14:8) and for good reason, which is revealed in Romans 8:26 (TPT):

> And in a similar way, the Holy Spirit takes hold of us in our human frailty to empower us in our weakness. For example, at times we don't even know how to pray, or know the best things to ask for. But the Holy Spirit rises up within us to super-intercede on our behalf, pleading to God with emotional sighs too deep for words.

An immediate benefit of praying in tongues is that we align our heart with God and pray His perfect will for our life. We often struggle in prayer because we don't know *what to pray* or *how to pray*. But when we're aided by God's Spirit, He prays for us, through us.

He knows what is taking place in the spirit realm, and as we yield to Him, He'll empower us to wage war effectively. Although our minds don't know what we're saying while our spirit prays, those moments are often accompanied by an overwhelming sense of peace and assurance.

Many times, while praying in tongues, my words and their tone change—they become more authoritative. I become aware that I'm engaged in warfare, and I'm using my authority to bring down enemy strongholds. In fact, the vision I shared at the start of this chapter was specifically in relation to praying in tongues.

Whenever we pray in the Spirit, we're praying into our destiny, paving a way to a breakthrough into our future. Don't ignore this wonderful gift that God's Spirit offers.

---

I encourage you to never give up praying!
What mountain stands in your way?
What doors are bolted shut?
What levels of destiny seem inaccessible to you?

You can break through them all by the power of prayer! Let's not remain idle; let's level up our prayers and see God do the impossible for us and through us.

# CHEAT CODE

### Remember

- Prayer is not just a way to receive from God—it's warfare!
- Breakthroughs are necessary to achieve leveling up.
- Intense, persistent, tenacious prayer brings kingdom breakthroughs on earth.
- *"God will trust us with greater breakthroughs when our heart desires to help others."*
- Praying in tongues aligns our heart with God's perfect will.

### Reflect

1. How would you describe your prayer life?

    \_\_\_\_"Ineffective. I find it hard to stay focused and committed to prayer."

    \_\_\_\_"Sometimes good, sometimes not so good. Depends on the day."

    \_\_\_\_"Fervent, vital. I love praying—it's a huge part of my life."

2. Explain your answer:

# 12

# THE ELEVATOR

*God Will Make a Way When There Seems No Way!*

What God originates—His plans and purposes—He'll orchestrate. What starts with God must also be sustained by Him. If we'll allow Him, God will lead us up to the peaks and heights of His plans and purposes. But this upward trajectory is not always linear. A mountainous landscape is not only made up of peaks to summit, but also valleys to pass through. The apostle Peter wrote:

> Therefore humble yourselves under the mighty hand of God [set aside self-righteous pride], so that He may exalt you [to a place of honor in His service] at the appropriate time, casting all your cares [all your anxieties, all your worries, and all your concerns, once and for all] on Him, for He cares about you [with deepest affection, and watches over you very carefully].
> (1 Peter 5:6–7 AMP)

God will show you *what* His plans for your life are, but He won't show you *how* they'll be fulfilled. You'll have to trust Him, which requires humbling yourself—submitting to God's way of doing things under His leadership. As you do, He'll promote you at the right time, exalting you to a place of honor in His service.

Will you trust Him? Or more importantly, can He trust you?

## Tested to Be Trusted

Part of the preparation process for a promotion to a level up involves going through tests to ensure that we can be trusted with greater levels of responsibility.

The idea of testing reminds me of something embarrassing—I used to be afraid to travel on airplanes. I'm not sure why, but fear gripped me every time I'd board a plane. (Maybe it was caused by all those 1980s action movies I watched growing up?) I used to travel with John Bevere as a personal assistant, taking care of tasks and offering him support as needed. This involved a lot of air travel.

On one occasion, we were on a four-day book tour through four different cities, and a friend of John's kindly offered his private jet for the trip. Honestly, it was a nice jet, but to me it felt like we were flying in a tin can with wings. During our flights, John could sense my apprehension, especially during takeoff.

In his kindness, John provided some relief for my fears. He shared that before a plane is released for widespread use, it first goes through a rigorous and exhaustive amount of testing. From the earliest stages of design, these tests are done to ensure its quality, performance, and reliability to transport passengers safely in a wide variety of weather conditions. Once the plane passes all the required tests, it's released for public use.

"This plane was tested; therefore, it can be trusted!" John told me. That brought me great comfort.

In a similar way, God takes us through a variety of tests before He promotes us. In our years in school, we were tested to show we were qualified to graduate. Our teachers and professors didn't examine us on material we didn't know; they tested us on the subjects we were taught.

And if we studied and prepared for their exams, we could confidently pass the tests.

In regard to the tests God gives us, John Bevere wrote, "We all have life-defining moments. They are like open-book tests, but often we don't know we have been examined until it is over."[21] So, if we're immersed in God's Word and consistently obeying His ways, we too can have confidence that we'll pass our "open-book" tests and move forward to our destiny.

If you're finding it difficult to believe that God will test you, then carefully examine this passage:

> Do you remember how the Lord led you through the wilderness for all those forty years, humbling you and *testing* you to find out how you would *respond*, and whether or not you would really obey him? (Deuteronomy 8:2 TLB)

God tested Israel during their wilderness season to find out if they'd obey Him. Their time in the wilderness was an important transition period designed to cleanse them from the wisdom and ways of Egypt while instilling into them God's wisdom and ways. God did this to prepare their hearts to possess the land they were destined to inherit. But judging by their response, they failed their tests. A whole generation, with the exception of two people, did not enter the Promised Land.

James the apostle understood the value of testing. He encouraged us to remain steadfast through the tests by keeping in mind the rewards that result from passing them. James shared:

> Blessed [happy, spiritually prosperous, favored by God] is the man who is steadfast under trial and perseveres when tempted; for when he has passed the test and been approved, he will receive the [victor's] crown of life which the Lord has promised to those who love Him." (James 1:12 AMP)

A stamp of approval is given to those who pass their tests, and they qualify for the victor's crown. In the ancient Greek language and culture, this crown represented victory and authority—not just for eternity, but also for here and now. According to the *Strong's Bible Dictionary*, the victor's crown also was considered a badge of royalty.

Today, that crown would be the equivalent to a VIP pass. In the past, athletes who won the victor's crown were given special access to exclusive places within their city. The application to us now is that when we successfully navigate challenges and difficulties—especially "sanctified experiences" orchestrated by God—we'll come out with greater authority in that area. This often leads to promotion, as the Lord can trust us with greater responsibility, which means access to exclusive places of our destiny.

Several years ago, I experienced a very difficult and trying season at Messenger when a leader really hurt me and my family. (For the record, this leader was not a Bevere.) When I found out about what was taking place, I brought it to the attention of my superiors. But this person lied and covered up what he'd done. For almost two years, I was left navigating the aftermath of what took place.

During this time, rarely did a day go by when I didn't break down in tears. For months, I lived with a broken heart and wrestled with anger, offense, rejection, and depression. There were many times when I had to resist the temptation to get revenge for the wrong done to me. Every day, I'd have to walk into the office and watch this person get praised, admired, and given opportunities I felt I deserved. I had to resist the urge to retaliate.

Through that season, God did a deep work in my heart. I learned valuable lessons about love, forgiveness, and trusting God. And, most importantly, I became closer to God.

One of the bigger lessons I learned was to trust God as my vindicator. As I committed my situation to Him, it forced me to look to Him for my help, not anyone else. What hurt the most during this time was that my leaders were unaware of what had really happened. I had no choice but to look to God to make things right.

Over time, I received the grace to forgive this man and also grew to the place where I could genuinely love him. I no longer desired harm against him, nor did I care if my leaders knew what he'd done. At this point, I had genuinely released my hurt and had committed my case to God. I desired the best for him and prayed for him and his family consistently, as if I were praying for myself. By the grace of God, I could be in his presence and still honor him as a leader.

Looking back, I'm grateful for the good that came out of this period of suffering. But I believe none of this would've been possible if I'd chosen to escape rather than walk through this season. And God knows there were several times I almost did. During that time, I was offered several job opportunities that were very appealing. I had well-meaning family and friends encouraging me to leave. But through it all, I kept sensing God saying, "Stay the course." Thankfully, I chose to handle things God's way, and passed many significant tests that later positioned me for a season of promise.

Toward the end of that time of testing, the Lord spoke the word "pivot" to me, indicating a turning point was about to occur. Within two weeks, the person who'd hurt me approached leadership, confessed his wrong, and the entirety of what had taken place was exposed. With the truth came vindication, as well as increased respect and trust for me with my leaders. In the weeks and months that followed, the Lord began to promote me in the workplace.

What's more, even the person who hurt me began a journey toward finding healing and wholeness. God had also done a work in his heart, and our leaders were so gracious to all of us. What the enemy meant for evil, God turned around for good—not just for me, but for all of us. This man went on to get his life in order and has since stepped into greater levels of success.

I believe the turning point in this whole scenario occurred the moment I genuinely chose to forgive. Forgiving the person who had done me wrong and continuing to serve him honorably allowed God to have His way. Through me, God was able to reveal His love toward this man—which ultimately positioned him to forgive himself. If I had not extended love and mercy toward him, not only would I have been held accountable, but things would've turned out differently.

As for me, I found healing through forgiveness and encountered the love of God in a transformative way. This situation taught me that God desired to do more than just vindicate me; He had the welfare of us all in mind.

When you're in the midst of testing, hold fast to God's Word and ways of doing things. This will ensure that you won't prolong your tests and have to repeat a level and maybe go around the same mountain again. During his unique testing process, Job confessed:

> "But he knows where I am going. And when he tests me, I will come out as pure as gold. For I have stayed on God's paths; I have followed his ways and not turned aside. I have not departed from his commands, but have treasured his words more than daily food. But once he has made his decision, who can change his mind? Whatever he wants to do, he does. So he will do to me whatever he has planned. He controls my destiny."
> (Job 23:10–14 NLT)

Job's words provide much needed insight for us to navigate our tests correctly. First, see beyond the test. Job encouraged himself, like James said, by keeping his focus on the reward: "I will come out as pure as gold." You, too, will come out, and you'll emerge better than the way you went in. Second, stay on God's paths and follow His ways. This means not departing from His words while treasuring them as your lifeline. The third and final thing, keep trusting God: "So he will do to me whatever he has planned. He controls my destiny" (Job 23:14 NLT).

Resist the urge to take matters into your own hands, and allow God to control your destiny. You may not understand all that you're going through now, but I promise it will all make sense later.

## Types of Tests

The types of tests we'll encounter vary, just like the way in which we're examined on a variety of subjects at school. Let's take a look at a few of these common tests we'll experience.

### The Character Test

> Until the time came to fulfill his dreams, the LORD tested Joseph's character. (Psalm 105:19 NLT)

Good character is foundational to sustain promotion. Otherwise, our gifts can take us places our character can't handle. We've all seen those who have shot to the top, but due to a lack of character, fell faster than they ascended. That's why character development is foundational to promotion. Legendary coach John Wooden said, "Ability may get you to the top, but it takes character to keep you there."

In between the time Joseph received dreams about his calling to the fulfillment of those dreams, his character was tested. These character tests included learning to forgive those who'd wronged him, avoiding sexual immorality, using his gifts to serve others, and learning to trust God in all things. As he remained faithful throughout his tests, Joseph experienced promotion.

> But he had already sent a man ahead of his people to Egypt; it was Joseph, who was sold as a slave. His feet were bruised by strong shackles and his soul was held by iron. God's promise to Joseph purged his character until it was time for his dreams to come true. Eventually, the king of Egypt sent for him, setting him free at last. Then Joseph was put in charge of everything under

the king; he became the master of the palace over all of the royal possessions. (Psalm 105:17–21 TPT)

When Joseph was promoted to prominence, he had the character to sustain it. As he stood on a balcony overlooking the land of Egypt, I'm sure Joseph had moments when he connected the dots and thought, *I'm living the dream. God is faithful. The dreams I dreamt years ago have now been fulfilled. They didn't happen the way I expected, but everything I went through was purposeful, and led me to where I am now.*

Joseph stayed the course to the promised completion. The Lord will do the same for you. Trust Him through the testing. You'll be thankful you did.

## The Faithfulness Test

The one who manages the little he has been given with faithfulness and integrity will be promoted and trusted with greater responsibilities. But those who cheat with the little they have been given will not be considered trustworthy to receive more. (Luke 16:10 TPT)

After my own season of testing, which I shared earlier in this chapter, I began to experience a time of promotion through being entrusted with greater responsibility to write and develop content on behalf of John and Lisa Bevere. On a particular day, John came into the office to participate in several meetings, but he first wanted to connect with me.

When he came to my office space, he shared that he had a pair of shoes he wanted to gift to me. As he gave me the box, he expressed, "Chris, I was given these shoes while in Singapore, and I knew I had to give them to you. And I just want to say thank you for the writing you're doing for me."

It was a kind gesture and meant a lot to me. When I opened the box, I found a pair of Adidas Ultra Boosts. Immediately, the Holy Spirit spoke to my heart and said, "Read the label on the shoe again." I read the words "Ultra Boost." He then said, "The season you've entered is a promotion. You've been faithful. And what you're doing now is an ultra-boost toward your destiny."

In a way, the shoes became a prophetic symbol that I was stepping into John's shoes and also was on the right path. I love how God can use things like that to speak to us and to remind us that nothing goes unnoticed with God.

Joseph was promoted and trusted with greater responsibilities because he passed the faithfulness test over and over again. He was faithful to serve his father, Jacob; his boss, Potiphar; and the prison guard. As a result, he became Pharaoh's right-hand man. I'm convinced that had Joseph not been faithful, he would've remained in prison.

To be faithful means to keep doing what's right, especially when you don't want to.

### The Motive Test

Motives matter to God. They're the reasons we do things. And God is most interested in *why* we do *what* we do: "We justify our actions by appearances; GOD examines our motives" (Proverbs 21:2 MSG).

Too often, impure motives are "justified" by righteous actions. When I began gaining leadership experience at my church in Australia, I received valuable growth experiences, especially in the area of my motives. Once, during a time of prayer, I was asking God to grow our youth ministry. My prayers were bold and passionate. And I was believing for God to draw youth into our church from the north, south, east, and west of Sydney.

While I was praying, the Holy Spirit interrupted me with a question. In my heart, I heard these words: "Why are you praying for growth?" First, is there anything wrong with praying for growth? Absolutely not. It's the right thing to do. However, God wanted to point something out in my heart that was wrong.

I responded, "I want to build the kingdom!"

The Holy Spirit immediately replied, "But whose kingdom are you building?"

At that moment, I paused with embarrassment as I realized the error of my heart. Deep down, I was more concerned about building a large youth ministry for my own benefit and reputation, not God's. It hurt.

> All the ways of a man are clean and innocent in his own eyes [and he may see nothing wrong in his actions], but the LORD weighs and examines the motives and intents [of the heart and knows the truth]. (Proverbs 16:2 AMP)

I wanted a large ministry because I thought it would add value and significance to my life. I'd attached my sense of worth to what I was attempting to achieve, rather than to my identity in God.

It was God's mercy and grace to point out my true motives. I repented and asked the Lord to purify my heart and help me build with the right motives. The change didn't happen immediately, but as I continued to align my heart with God's heart for the youth, eventually my heart changed also.

Part of the testing process is for us to see what's truly in our heart. God already knows, but we often don't. Tests expose us, but they also give us an opportunity to grow and change. How we respond determines whether we grow or not.

The apostle Paul experienced a variety of tests before he was approved and trusted as a messenger of God. He confessed:

> God tested us thoroughly to make sure we were qualified to be trusted with this Message. Be assured that when we speak to you we're not after crowd approval—only God approval. Since we've been put through that battery of tests, you're guaranteed that both we and the Message are free of error, mixed motives, or hidden agendas. We never used words to butter you up. No

one knows that better than you. And God knows we never used words as a smoke screen to take advantage of you. (1 Thessalonians 2:3–5 MSG)

Paul could guarantee to his followers that his message was free from error, mixed motives, and hidden agendas because of the battery of tests he'd passed. His motives had been tested; therefore, he could be trusted.

If our motives are not correctly dealt with and aligned, they could lead us astray. The Bible says, "mixed motives twist life into tangles; pure motives take you straight down the road" (Proverbs 21:8 MSG).

Confusion in life is often the result of conflicting motives. Gehazi, who was Elisha's servant and destined to become his successor, wrestled with mixed motives. His struggles were revealed after he witnessed Elisha's involvement with a miracle healing of the Syrian military commander named Naaman who was suffering from leprosy.

Elisha had told Naaman to dip himself seven times in the Jordan River to be cleansed of his disease. And he was! Naaman, filled with gratitude for his healing, offered Elisha a large amount of silver and choice clothing. But Elisha politely refused to accept the gifts and sent Naaman and his servants off with a blessing.

This is when Gehazi became undone. While Naaman was still on his way back home, we read:

> But he hadn't gone far when Gehazi, servant to Elisha the Holy Man, said to himself, "My master has let this Aramean Naaman slip through his fingers without so much as a thank-you. By the living GOD, I'm going after him to get something or other from him!" And Gehazi took off after Naaman.
> (2 Kings 5:19–21 MSG)

At this point, it's obvious that Gehazi was in ministry for what he could get out of it, not for what he could give. He couldn't possibly allow Naaman to leave without being compensated. (What a stark contrast to what we saw with Paul!) Gehazi disobeyed Elisha's wishes, pursued Naaman, and got what he wanted—and more when he returned home:

> He returned and stood before his master. Elisha said, "So what have you been up to, Gehazi?" "Nothing much," he said. Elisha said, "Didn't you know I was with you in spirit when that man stepped down from his chariot to greet you? Tell me, is this a time to look after yourself, lining your pockets with gifts? Naaman's skin disease will now infect you and your family, with no relief in sight." Gehazi walked away, his skin flaky and white like snow. (2 Kings 5:25–27 MSG)

Gehazi was called out. His motives were exposed. Sadly, many like Gehazi, have succumbed to the allure of wealth and riches. I, too, have often been tempted to take opportunity simply for the prospect of a greater income—maybe that's happened to you, too. There's nothing wrong with desiring to earn more money and provide for yourself and your family, but when the desire for money interferes with obedience to God, then it's a problem.

That's what caused Judas to betray Jesus, and that's what causes many to fail their motive test—they're more concerned about what they can get from obeying God than simply pleasing God.

It's easy to justify or cover up impure motives by works that "appear" righteous and good. But please don't forget: God is more interested in *why* we do *what* we do. Man looks at the outward appearance; God looks at the heart.

### The Trust Test

> But I am trusting you, O LORD, saying, "You are my God!" My future is in your hands. (Psalm 31:14–15 NLT)

Trusting God requires committing your future into His hands. That's why these words from David's psalm have encouraged me throughout my upward journey. Too many times I've tried to take matters into my own hands and failed miserably. In those moments, I've realized I was doing things my way, not God's. The Bible tells us clearly:

> Trust GOD from the bottom of your heart; don't try to figure out everything on your own. Listen for GOD's voice in everything you do, everywhere you go; he's the one who will keep you on track. (Proverbs 3:5 MSG)

Trusting God means that, at times, we won't understand His ways of doing things. Without this uncertainty, trust won't be necessary. Yet despite uncertainty, we can be certain that God is good, and His plans for us are for good. In the words of Corrie ten Boom, "We can trust an unknown future to a known God."

## Promotion Comes from God

> This I know: the favor that brings promotion and power doesn't come from anywhere on earth, for no one exalts a person but God, the true judge of all. He alone determines where favor rests. He anoints one for greatness and brings another down to his knees. (Psalm 75:6–7 TPT)

God is the One who promotes. Throughout history, many great names and nations have risen and fallen. Some are remembered, most are forgotten. Although we have a variety of manmade systems and procedures that determine how promotion occurs, God controls them all.

In regard to this, we're told, "It's as easy for God to steer a king's heart for his purposes as it is for him to direct the course of a stream" (Proverbs 21:1 TPT). It's truly amazing how God's sovereignty is evident everywhere:

Not only can He see the heart of all; He can also steer the heart of all.

Here are a few examples from Scripture of God's wisdom and sovereignty in regard to promotion:

*God raised up Pharaoh.* He used the stubbornness of an evil ruler as a catalyst to redeem the children of Israel from bondage. Through this display of power, the Lord's fame spread throughout the nations of the then-known world:

> For the Scripture says to the Pharaoh, "For this very purpose I have raised you up, that I may show My power in you, and that My name may be declared in all the earth." (Romans 9:17)

*God raised up Joshua.* What God had started with Moses, He continued through Joshua. Joshua had faithfully served Moses in private, and the Lord had prepared him to be exalted publicly. He would lead Israel to possess the Promised Land:

> And the LORD said to Joshua, "This day I will begin to exalt you in the sight of all Israel, that they may know that, as I was with Moses, *so* I will be with you. (Joshua 3:7)

*God raised up David.* When it was time for a successor to replace King Saul, God personally found David, a man after His own heart, to be king. God even made sure that Samuel anointed the right person, the one He had chosen for Himself:

> God also chose his beloved one, David. He promoted him from caring for sheep and made him his prophetic servant. (Psalm 78:70 TPT)

*God raised up Cyrus.* Centuries before he was born, God spoke of how King Cyrus would arise and play a pivotal role in relation to God's dealings with Israel:

I will raise up Cyrus to fulfill my righteous purpose, and I will guide his actions. He will restore my city and free my captive people—without seeking a reward! I, the LORD of Heaven's Armies, have spoken!" (Isaiah 45:13 NLT)

*God raised up the apostle Paul.* A man who once persecuted the church would eventually become one of its pillars—building the very people he initially sought to destroy:

But the Master said, "Don't argue. Go! I have picked him as my personal representative to non-Jews and kings and Jews. And now I'm about to show him what he's in for—the hard suffering that goes with this job." (Acts 9:15–16 MSG)

After reviewing these examples, it's evident who's in control! God is very much involved with the affairs of mankind. Whether it's Israel, the church, or other nations—it's obvious God is actively at work behind the scenes.

## Many Are Called, Few Are Chosen

God's calling on your life is an invitation to take part in the unfolding of His story. Just like Joseph, Pharaoh, Joshua, David, Cyrus, and Paul all played their part, you too are to have a role in the outworking of God's plans and purposes for mankind. However, your response to His call will determine what happens next.

Sadly, not everyone is willing to respond to this invitation. On two specific occasions, Jesus expressed, "'many are called but few [are] chosen'" (Matthew 20:16; 22:14). His words reveal that there's a clear distinction between being *called* and being *chosen*. Another word for "chosen" is "commissioned." Your calling begins the process that ultimately leads to being commissioned. Not all who are called make it to their commissioning, because not all pass their tests, complete their preparation, and stay the course.

A closer look at Jesus's statements lends even greater clarity. His first reference relates to an incorrect attitude toward how God rewards His laborers. The second reference relates to the failure to adequately prepare oneself. Jesus's parable concerns a person the king had invited to his son's wedding who failed to meet the required dress code.

When this invited person was confronted about his outfit, he seemed completely unaware and taken aback. The main point Jesus was communicating was that there are many called to serve God, but due to *an incorrect attitude* and *a lack of preparation*, they fail to qualify for their commissioning.

Our attitude to His call, and our cooperation with Him as He works in our life, set the pace for what He'll do with us. Once we respond to His call and make ourselves available to Him, He begins to prepare us for what He's called us to do.

Here's how this occurred in the life of Paul:

> The congregation in Antioch was blessed with a number of prophet-preachers and teachers: Barnabas, Simon, nicknamed Niger, Lucius the Cyrenian, Manaen, an advisor to the ruler Herod, Saul. One day as they were worshiping God—they were also fasting as they waited for guidance—the Holy Spirit spoke: "Take Barnabas and Saul and commission them for the work I have called them to do." (Acts 13:1–3 MSG)

Paul was called to be an apostle, but he wasn't commissioned to this office immediately. According to biblical scholars, it took approximately fourteen to seventeen years between the time he was called as an apostle to the time he was commissioned.

In order to level up into the fullness of our calling, we must succeed in a series of tests and challenges. Unfortunately, many are called, but only a few are chosen. Let's be numbered among those who level up all the way and lay hold of all that God has destined for us to do and receive.

### Waymaker

> "I will march out in front of you and level every obstacle. I will shatter to pieces bronze doors and slice through iron bars."
> (Isaiah 45:2 TPT)

God has gone before you to make a way for you to level up. And He's not just a step ahead—He's years ahead, knowing the end from the beginning. He's divinely orchestrated people, circumstances, and events to work in your favor.

It's easier to grasp this truth when looking back, but we'll have to accept it by faith when looking ahead. Like a master chess player, He has already planned His moves ahead of time. Now it's up to you to allow Him to position you correctly.

Over the course of this book, we've discussed how life is lived on levels. I hope you've been challenged and encouraged to keep growing so you can shift from where you have potential to where you are potent, fulfilling your destiny.

I urge you to remain committed to the upward journey. As you make progress, keep in mind that it's not enough to be full of potential, unless it's being realized.

There's an upward call beckoning to you. Will you answer it?

# CHEAT CODE

### Remember

- "God will show you *what* His plans for your life are, but He won't necessarily show you *how* they'll be fulfilled."
- Successfully passing life tests means we can be trusted with greater levels of responsibility.
- During testing, hold fast to God's Word and ways of doing things.
- Tests are of three types: Character, Faithfulness, and Motives.
- God goes before you to make a way for you to Level Up!

### Reflect

1. I've identified these types of tests: *Character. Faithfulness. Motives.* Which of these tests are you struggling to pass in your spiritual journey?
2. In what areas of your life do you want God to be a Waymaker so you will better love and serve Him?
3. What parts of the "Level Up" message have influenced you the most? How is what you've learned reshaping your growth process?

# ACKNOWLEDGMENTS

The book you hold in your hands is a team effort, so I'd love to acknowledge those who contributed to it:

**John Bevere**: I'll never forget the day you met with me in your office and asked me to write this book. It was a pivotal moment in my life. We connected on a heart level as you embraced me as a son (and yes, I cried). I love you . . . so much! Thank you for believing in me!

**Addison Bevere**: Words cannot express both the impact and the influence you've had in my life. Not only have you championed me as a writer and have supported this message, you've also helped me grow as a man and as a leader. Thank you for not giving up on me!

**Erwin McManus, Ed Mylett, Donald Miller, and Phil Pringle**: Each of your messages have greatly impacted mine. I'm forever grateful for your influence.

**Bruce Nygren, Cory Emberson, Laura Willbur, and Bonnie Olsen**: Thank you for ensuring the grammar, punctuation, and style of this message was excellent and congruent. You are the game changers!

**The Messenger International Design team**: Joe, Bryson, Allie, you guys challenged me and took this project to new levels! Thank you for investing your hearts and gifts into your work. I'm grateful to labor alongside you.

**Holy Spirit**: You worked this message *in me* before you released it *through me*. Thank You for giving me the grace to not only share this message, but to also live it.

# ENDNOTES

1. Online Dictionary: https://www.google.com/search?client=firefox-b-1-d&q=potent+meaning
2. A.W. Tozer, *The Pursuit of God*. 2015 (Abbotsford, Wisconsin: Aneko Press, Updated Edition 2015).
3. https://www.quotes.net/quote/38411
4. https://www.youtube.com/watch?v=fTY4-71Vf_I
5. T.D. Jakes, *Destiny: Step into Your Purpose*, Kindle Edition (Nashville: FaithWords, 2016), 223–224.
6. R.A. Montgomery, *Journey Under the Sea: Choose Your Own Adventure* (New York: Bantam Books, 1982).
7. https://news.stanford.edu/2005/06/14/jobs-061505/
8. C.S. Lewis, *Prince Caspian: The Chronicles of Narnia* (New York: HarperCollins, 2002).
9. Andy Stanley, *Visioneering: God's Blueprint for Developing and Maintaining Vision* (Colorado Springs: Multnomah Books, 1999).
10. Anders Ericsson, *Peak: Secrets from the New Science of Expertise* (Boston: Mariner Books, 2017).
11. John C. Maxwell, *Talent Is Never Enough: Discover the Choices That Will Take You Beyond Your Talent* (Nashville: Thomas Nelson, 2007).
12. Kevin Hall, *Aspire: Discovering Your Purpose Through the Power of Words*, Reprint edition (New York: HarperCollins e-books, 2009).
13. https://www.brainyquote.com/quotes/ralph_waldo_emerson_134898
14. https://www.brainyquote.com/quotes/mark_twain_141714
15. Steven Pressfield, *The War of Art: Winning the Inner Creative Battle* (New York: Black Irish Entertainment, 2012).
16. Marianne Williamson, *A Return to Love: Reflections on the Principles of "A Course in Miracles"* (New York: Harper Perennial, Reissue 1996).
17. *Rocky Balboa* (2006), written and directed by Sylvester Stallone. https://www.youtube.com/watch?v=D_Vg4uyYwEk

18. Malcolm Gladwell, *David and Goliath: Underdogs, Misfits, and the Art of Battling Giants* (New York: Little, Brown and Company, 2013).
19. E.M. Bounds, *E.M. Bounds on Prayer* (Peabody, MA: Hendrickson Publishers, Kindle Edition, 2006).
20. Story based on author's experience and research.
21. John Bevere, *Honor's Reward: Unlocking the Power of This Forgotten Virtue* (Palmer Lake, CO: Messenger International, 2019).

# Free Courses, Audiobooks & More to Help You Grow in Your Faith.

MessengerX is a revolutionary tool that connects you with world-class teachers, authors, and leaders who will help you embrace a vibrant faith in your everyday life.

Scan the QR code to dowload MessengerX

# STAY CONNECTED

**On Social Media:**

 @ChrisPaceOfficial

 @ChrisPaceOfficial

**For Speaking Engagements:**

 cpace@messengerintl.org

 Tel: (719) 487-3000
Intl: (800) 648-1477

# LOVED READING LEVEL UP?
# GIVE IT AWAY!

If reading this book impacted you and you'd like more copies for those in your sphere of influence (perhaps your church, small group, company, friends, or family), please reach out to my team at:

**mail@messengerinternational.org** or
**(800) 648-1477** to get a discount on a bulk order!